CW01081670

2 to 22 D[A]
IN
NEW ENGLAND

THE ITINERARY PLANNER

ANNE E. WRIGHT

John Muir Publications
Santa Fe, New Mexico

Originally published as *22 Days in New England*

For Randy, without whom this book would not have been possible.

Special thanks to my parents, Linda, and Gail, for their research assistance, and to Richard Harris for his support and guidance throughout the project.

John Muir Publications, P.O. Box 613, Santa Fe, NM 87504
© 1989, 1991, 1992, 1993, 1994 by Anne E. Wright
Cover and maps © 1989, 1991, 1992, 1993, 1994 by John Muir Publications
All rights reserved.
Printed in the United States of America
First printing January 1994.

ISSN 1059-2962
ISBN 1-56261-135-6

Cover photo Leo de Wys Inc./Fridmar Damm
Maps Randy Johnson
Typography Ken Wilson
Printer Banta Company

Distributed to the book trade by
W. W. Norton & Company, Inc.
New York, New York

CONTENTS

2 to 22 Days in New England

HOW TO USE THIS BOOK

Your New England tour begins in Boston, Massachusetts, one of the nation's oldest cities, and ends there three weeks later after a 1,200-mile loop through some of the nation's most scenic and historically significant terrain. Although this may not seem like a lot of ground to cover during the course of your vacation, believe me, your 2 to 22 days will be chock-full of engaging activities, adventures, and picturesque sights.

New England is the birthplace of our nation in many respects. The pilgrims landed here in 1620, the first battle of the Revolutionary War was fought on Massachusetts soil, Harvard University in Cambridge is the cornerstone of American education, and founding fathers such as John Adams spent their lives here. You'll feel history all around you as you pause on centuries-old town greens, drive past crusty stone walls that define property lines, ramble over covered bridges, and visit time-weathered historic homes and monuments. Along the way, you'll see where Shakers worshiped, poets penned, colonists rebelled, whalers toiled, and presidents were born.

Nature has endowed New England with a beautiful landscape. Atlantic currents and ice age glaciers have sculpted this part of the country to near-perfection. During your holiday you'll have the opportunity to stretch out on sparkling white sand beaches, picnic in rocky coves, watch playful seals in their natural habitat, hike pine-covered trails, stand atop the highest peak in the Northeast, swim in bubbling mountain streams, and dine on fish recently snatched from the ocean while breathing in the salty sea air. If you're lucky, you'll also see the hills ablaze with vibrant colors as winter approaches.

This guide opens the door to your New England adventure. It has been organized for quick reference in an itinerary format divided into 22 daily sections containing:

1. A **suggested schedule** for each day's travel and sightseeing.

2. A detailed **travel route** description for each driving segment of your trip.

3. **Sightseeing highlights** (rated in order of importance: ▲▲▲ Don't miss; ▲▲ Try hard to see; and ▲ See if you get the chance).

4. **Lodging**, **campground**, and **restaurant** suggestions for each night of the trip.

5. **Helpful Hints**—random tidbits that will help your trip run smoothly.

6. **Itinerary Options**—excursion suggestions for travelers who have extra time.

7. User-friendly **maps** designed to show you what the road up ahead is really like.

Why 2 to 22 Days?

For those who have about three weeks of vacation this year, 2 to 22 Days itinerary guidebooks can help you use that time to the fullest extent by directing you to the best a region has to offer. How often have you wasted precious time off just trying to locate a decent restaurant or missed out on a treasured museum because you spent too much time in a disappointing one? In *2 to 22 Days in New England*, I've done the legwork for you so that your holiday will be as trouble-free and enjoyable as possible.

The itinerary, my ideal trip, includes a sampling of sights everyone should experience on a visit to New England, personal favorite haunts, and a realistic time frame in which to see them all. The daily schedules will help you structure your days but are not carved in stone. Use them flexibly to create the best trip for you. For instance, if art history is not your thing, skip the Boston Museum of Fine Arts on Day 2 and go to the Computer Museum instead, or spend the afternoon gorging on Fenway Franks at a Red Sox game.

What if you have less than 22 days? No problem. One of the nicest things about *2 to 22 Days in New England* is its adaptability. The itinerary is created for those who have three weeks, but if you only have one, pick the week that interests you the most.

The route begins and ends in Boston because it is the easiest point of entry for those traveling to New England from afar; however, the itinerary can be joined anywhere. Given the compactness of New England, no stop on the itinerary is more than a 3½-hour drive from Boston, with the exception of Bar Harbor, which is about 6 hours. Those living in or near Boston can certainly use two- and three-day segments of the trip for a number of weekend getaways.

When to Go

This itinerary is designed for travel between mid-May and mid-September. Many historical sites, restaurants, and hotels listed are only open during those months when the climate is at its best. Of course, New England is known worldwide for its spectacular fall foliage, which generally reaches its peak in Vermont and New Hampshire in early October. Winter skiing is also a popular attraction there. Do keep in mind that if you visit New England for the foliage or for skiing, many of the suggested sightseeing highlights will already be closed for the season.

July and August are the busiest months in terms of tourists, and the most expensive—particularly in the coastal regions. Vermont and New Hampshire are naturally very crowded during peak leaf-peeping season, when places like North Conway in the Mt. Washington valley of New Hampshire turn into veritable parking lots on Columbus Day weekend. If you plan to travel during peak periods, advance lodging reservations are a necessity. I've been told that churches have had to open their doors to stranded tourists, or worse, weary travelers have spent frosty New England nights upright in their cars. For your trip to run as smoothly as possible, I recommend calling ahead for reservations.

Personally, I think September is the best time to see New England. The weather is usually sunny and pleasant without the heat and humidity of July and August, ocean temperatures are at their warmest, and many sites are still operating on their extended summer schedules. You may miss the foliage at its peak (although I'll bet you'll see a few leaves turning in the northern regions), but you'll also miss many of the summer tourists, and off-season rates begin just after Labor Day in some coastal towns.

June is another good time to travel and avoid the crowds, but the weather is less predictable than in September, and high-season rates generally go into effect on Memorial Day weekend.

Transportation

Just about all of the principal airlines have several daily nonstop flights to Boston from most major U.S. airports. Prices vary depending upon your departure city, but fares from airline to airline are generally comparable. Your travel agent can help get you the lowest-price flight available for your desired departure date. It is usually best to purchase your ticket at least 30 days in advance to secure the lowest fare.

While the metropolitan Boston area is readily accessible by public transportation and a network of commuter trains and buses, the rest of the trip is not. Greyhound, Bonanza, Peter Pan, and Vermont Transit bus companies serve the more rural areas of the itinerary to some extent, but you will find it hard to travel to all the sights once you reach each destination by bus.

This trip is designed for those traveling by car, RV, or motorcycle. With the exception of Sargent Drive along Somme Sound in Maine, all suggested routes are open to those types of vehicles. However, the auto roads to Cadillac Summit in Acadia National Park and to Mt. Washington in New Hampshire may be too precarious for larger motor homes.

For aesthetic reasons, this suggested route follows secondary highways rather than major interstates in most cases. This means your average driving speed will be 45 to 50 miles per hour rather than 55 or 65. Distances between New England destinations are relatively short when compared to other parts of the country, so speed and travel time are not major factors in trip planning. You'll be able to appreciate the surrounding countryside better at slower speeds. You'll also find that states such as

Maine, New Hampshire, and Vermont are very good about marking historical sites, lodging, and eating establishments that are off these secondary roads with directional and mileage signs.

Renting a Vehicle

All major car rental agencies have offices in Boston. Compact cars rent for about $200 per week with 700 to 1,000 free miles weekly. Subcompacts are somewhat cheaper and get better gas mileage but can feel cramped when you spend a lot of time inside them.

Traveling by rental recreational vehicle is another possible way to explore New England. A 20-foot RV sleeping up to five people rents for about $680 weekly during June, $940 during July and August, and $415 during the winter months. These base rates don't include add-on charges for collision insurance, vehicle preparation, propane, and the like. In the Boston area, RVs can be rented from West Suburban Leasing at 70 Prospect Street in Somerville. Call them at (617) 437-7500 for rental information, or contact their parent company, Cruise America, toll-free at (800)327-7778. Keep in mind that while touring by RV is a convenient way to travel, renting one will only mean significant lodging savings if you are traveling with more than two people.

Lodging

Country inns are one of the best ways to truly immerse yourself in New England tradition. Inns, some of which have been operating for 100 years or more, serve regional specialties, are often furnished with priceless antiques, and generally offer comfortable to exceptional lodging, sometimes at little more than the cost of a motel room. A night in a country inn averages about $90 for two during the summer and about $60 off-season. In many cases, the room rate includes a full breakfast, making the cost more appealing. Motels in the area average about $55 for two but often provide only half as much in the way of amenities and atmosphere. However, if you're traveling with a family, motels may be the only affordable lodging other

than camping. For those who really want to travel lavishly,
I have also listed luxury accommodations.

Camping is a much cheaper alternative to staying in
either bed and breakfasts or motels, although many campgrounds on the itinerary are not as convenient to the
sights. Campgrounds operated by state, national, and
municipal park services usually charge less than private
campgrounds—about $10 to $12 per night. Park-run
campgrounds tend to be more wooded and less crowded
than private ones but often don't have facilities such as
hot showers, grocery stores, playgrounds, or swimming
pools on the premises as many private camping areas do.
Of course, there is a price to pay for convenience: nightly
rates at private campgrounds run at least $15—or more.
To get the most satisfaction from your trip, choose the
type of lodging that best suits your life-style and budget.

Food
Preparing your own meals is the most economical way to
eat on your trip, and you shouldn't have any trouble finding adequate provisions at any point along the way. If
you're not equipped for food preparation or prefer to
leave that task to others while on vacation, be prepared to
spend an average of at least $3 to $5 for breakfast, $5 for
lunch, and $10 for dinner, per person, when eating out.
The restaurants I suggest are ones that I've personally
enjoyed, or that have local reputations for their food quality, uniqueness, convenience, or price. Fresh seafood is
what comes to mind first when one thinks of New
England cuisine, but places like Boston and Cambridge
offer the visitor a wide variety in ethnic dining as well.

An ice chest or a disposable styrofoam cooler, stocked
with soda, juice, yogurt, cheese, and other snacks, can
save both money and time. If your bed and breakfast
sends you off with a hearty morning meal, you can often
get by until dinner with just a yogurt in the early afternoon. If your lodging establishment doesn't provide
breakfast, a chilled fruit cup from the cooler may be just
the thing to start the day. By cutting out one restaurant
meal a day, you can reduce the total trip cost by more

than $100 per person. Having the cooler will also save time since you won't have to pull off the highway every time you feel a pang of hunger or thirst. Besides, the less time you spend dining, the more time you'll have to explore the New England you came to see.

Licenses

Since campfire and fishing regulations vary from state to state, it is wise to check with each state prior to engaging in either activity. Most states require fishing licenses (Maine sells theirs at the Tourist Information Center in Kittery), and in some areas, permits are required for campfires.

What to Bring

Mark Twain once said, "One of the brightest gems in the New England weather is the dazzling uncertainty of it." There couldn't be a truer statement, so the best way to deal with New England weather is to come prepared. Even in the hottest summer months, it is possible to run into cool evenings in parts of Maine, Vermont, and New Hampshire. Bring at least one heavy sweater no matter what season you plan to visit the area. The sweater will also come in handy any time you are out on the Atlantic, whether it's on a whale-watching vessel, the ferry to Nantucket, or a small pleasure craft; the ocean breezes can be quite chilling.

Although I hope you won't have occasion to use it, rain-gear is a must when traveling through New England. It is unlikely that you'll be able to spend three weeks there without encountering some form of precipitation, even if it is only a soft island mist on Martha's Vineyard. I recommend packing a lightweight hooded poncho to use while cycling or hiking and a fold-up umbrella for city sightseeing.

Binoculars will help bring the scenic vistas and wildlife of Acadia and the White Mountains National Forest into closer view, so make room in your suitcase for a pair. You wouldn't want to miss seeing the seals basking on the rocks just off the Maine coast.

Also pack a small empty knapsack or day-pack. It should be large enough to hold your sweater, poncho, guidebook, map, camera, and binoculars but lightweight enough to carry easily on your back. You'll find it invaluable when hiking, traveling to the islands, or simply transporting a picnic lunch.

Recommended Reading

Reading (or rereading) *The House of Seven Gables* by Nathaniel Hawthorne, *Little Women* by Louisa May Alcott, *Ethan Frome* by Edith Wharton, and *Walden* by Henry David Thoreau will complement your New England sojourn as you visit the haunts and homes that inspired these great American literary classics. The many layers of Newport, Rhode Island, society were the basis for Thornton Wilder's enjoyable *Theophilus North*, while Henry Beston spent a Thoreau-like year in a tiny house on Nauset Beach in Cape Cod recording the passage of nature in his book, *The Outermost House*; either book will add an extra dimension to your trip. Robert McCloskey's *Make Way for Ducklings*, a delightful tale of a duck family living in the Boston Public Gardens, will help the city come alive for young children.

As a supplemental guidebook, *The Complete Guide to Bed & Breakfasts, Inns & Guesthouses in the United States and Canada* by Pamela Lanier will help you locate that perfect country inn. Fodor's New England guide is a good background information source for those who wish to stray from the 22-day itinerary.

DAY 1 Arrive in Boston and get settled in your hotel. Then put on your walking shoes. Today you'll visit the USS *Constitution*, Old North Church, Paul Revere's House, and the Bunker Hill Monument—all stops on Boston's renowned Freedom Trail. Round out the day browsing through Quincy Market's smart shops, sampling delicacies from the Market's main food hall, strolling along the nearby waterfront, and dining in one of the area's restaurants.

DAY 2 Today you'll explore Boston's museums: Isabella Stewart Gardner's Venetian Palazzo and the Museum of Fine Arts are two of the city's most beautiful. At sunset, get a bird's-eye view of the city from the Hancock observation deck, and have a late dinner along posh Newbury Street.

DAY 3 Cross the Charles River to Boston's sister city, Cambridge, and bustling Harvard Square. Harvard University's outstanding museums await art, history, and science devotees, or you may prefer to saunter through the college's ivied courtyards or amble past Brattle Street's stately homes, including that of poet Henry Wadsworth Longfellow.

DAY 4 Travel to historic Concord to stand on the site of the first battle of the Revolutionary War. Take in colonial period rooms at the Concord Museum or visit the home of writer Louisa May Alcott. Picnic at Thoreau's Walden Pond; then it's on to Lexington for the Museum of Our National Heritage.

DAY 5 There is more to hunt than witches in the beguiling city of Salem, and today you will unearth some of the city's hidden treasures.

DAY 6 Driving along Massachusetts' "other cape," Cape Ann, you'll see the eccentric Hammond Castle and the fishing port of Gloucester, lunch by the sea in the artist colony of Rockport, and then continue up the coast to Kennebunk, Maine.

DAY 7 Today you'll travel a large portion of Maine's celebrated coastline, passing through the picturesque villages of Camden, Rockport, and Wiscasset, to reach Bar Harbor by evening.

DAY 8 Glorious vistas atop Cadillac Mountain and the pounding Atlantic surf await you today in Acadia National Park, the easternmost U.S. national park.

DAY 9 Give Acadia and Bar Harbor a last lingering look before you proceed across central Maine. After you pass through Gorham Notch, the scenic panorama of New Hampshire's Presidential Range from Mt. Washington's summit is the high point of the day. Late afternoon is for unwinding in Jackson or poking through shops and factory outlets in nearby North Conway.

DAY 10 Beautiful scenery abounds as you continue through the White Mountain National Forest. You'll see Crawford and Franconia notches and the Old Man of the Mountain and perhaps hike the Flume Trail. Stop for the night in charming Woodstock, Vermont.

DAY 11 Enjoy Vermont's Green Mountains, picturesque villages, maple syrup, and delicious cheddar cheese.

DAY 12 Spend the day in the college towns of Bennington and Williamstown, viewing folk art by Grandma Moses in the morning and French impressionist works, among others, in the afternoon.

DAY 13 The spartan life of the Shakers at Hancock Shaker Village makes an interesting contrast to the more traditional American life-style depicted in colorful oils at the Norman Rockwell Museum in Stockbridge. Today you will observe both. A classical concert at Tanglewood or a modern dance performance at Jacob's Pillow caps off a memorable day in the Berkshires.

DAY 14 Travel southeast from Stockbridge into Connecticut and follow the Connecticut River valley, making stops in Hartford, the state's capital, and the river towns of East Haddam and Essex. The night will be spent in the coastal town of Mystic.

DAY 15 Take a trip back through maritime history with a visit to the nation's largest maritime museum, Mystic Seaport. Then let yourself be entertained by thousands of aquatic creatures at Mystic's Marinelife Aquarium.

DAY 16 To get a glimpse of the greener grass on the other side of the fence, tour Rosecliff or the palatial Breakers, two examples of the lavish summer "cottages" built at the turn of the century by wealthy families such as the Vanderbilts. After the mansions, get a fresh breath of salty sea air along the Cliff Walk, or stroll Newport's downtown wharf area where boutiques and boats entice the visitor.

DAY 17 Depart for Cape Cod, stopping along the way in the whaling port of New Bedford. Visit Heritage Plantation and Sandwich Glass Museum in Sandwich, Cape Cod's oldest town.

DAYS 18 and 19 Spend these two days bicycling, beachcombing, and window-shopping on the islands of Nantucket and Martha's Vineyard.

DAY 20 Return to Cape Cod and travel its length to artsy Provincetown. Explore the spectacular sand dunes of the National Seashore along the way.

DAY 21 You'll travel from spirited Provincetown, along Cape Cod's scenic Route 6A, to historic Plymouth, the site of the Pilgrims' first settlement.

DAY 22 Return to Boston to end your three-week journey where it began, stopping in South Shore seaside villages and at the John F. Kennedy Memorial Library along the way.

BOSTON

Your New England tour begins in New England's largest city, and one of the nation's oldest—Boston, Massachusetts.

Suggested Schedule

9:30 a.m.	Visit the Public Gardens.
10:00 a.m.	Begin your all-day tour of Boston's Freedom Trail.
1:00 p.m.	Lunch in the Italian North End.
2:00 p.m.	Cross over to Charlestown on the Freedom Trail to visit the USS *Constitution* and Bunker Hill Monument.
5:30 p.m.	End your day browsing in Quincy Market's smart shops, then dining in one of the area's restaurants.

Arriving in Boston

Although Logan Airport is only 2½ miles from downtown Boston, getting to the downtown area can often be an exhausting experience. If you're renting a car, *don't* pick it up at the airport. Wait until Day 4 when you are ready to leave the city and begin your trip up the coast. Cab fare into the city will run at least $10 and can be very expensive if you get stuck in traffic, which you're bound to do. But a taxi may be your only option if you have a lot of luggage. Share a cab if possible. (Some downtown hotels will pick up guests from the airport, so you may want to call and check with your lodging to see if they offer such a service before jumping into a taxi.)

If you are traveling light, the MBTA (Massachusetts Bay Transportation Authority) is the fastest and least expensive means to reach the downtown area. A free shuttle bus that stops regularly at all airline terminals will take you to the Blue Line subway stop. A subway token is 85 cents, and in ten minutes you'll be in the heart of Boston. Board the train on the "Inbound" side of the tracks. A map of the entire subway system is clearly posted in every subway station to help guide you to your destination.

Another option when traveling to downtown is to take the Water Taxi from Logan Airport. This is a quick and scenic method, but unless your hotel is located on the waterfront, you'll still have to transfer to some other mode of transportation once across the harbor.

Amtrak trains arrive at South Station several times a day from New York and points south. South Station is on the main subway line, and no doubt your hotel will only be a short subway or cab ride away.

Greyhound operates a terminal in the city, providing access to Boston from many smaller towns. The depot is near the Arlington Street subway stop of the Green Line in Back Bay.

By car, Boston can be reached from the west by the Massachusetts Turnpike, from the north by Interstate 95 to Route 1, and from the northwest and south by Interstate 93 (the southern portion just below Boston is locally known as the Southeast Expressway).

Getting Around

Walking is the preferable form of transportation in this compact city. Be sure to wear comfortable shoes, since many of the old brick and cobblestone streets were in place long before high heels came into vogue.

The subway system is the oldest in the country and sometimes operates like an antique. The network of lines (Red, Green, Blue, and Orange) is quite extensive in the heart of the city, but check your street map before hopping on the system. Often three stops on the subway are only three physical blocks apart, and it would take more time to wait for the train than to walk the distance yourself. The farther one travels from the city center, the more it makes sense to travel by subway, but it is best to avoid subway travel at rush hour. Tokens are 85 cents each, and in some areas, additional fare is required. Subway stations are marked by a "T" symbol. If you plan to use the subway often, short term visitor passes can be purchased at the Greater Boston Convention & Visitor's Bureau at the Prudential Tower, or ask at any MBTA office for additional sales locations.

Since Boston has been settled for more than 350 years, a great number of existing thoroughfares were laid down over old cowpaths that follow no logical pattern. The haphazard network of streets can be confusing to out-of-towners, and parking spaces are hard to come by. Don't try to demystify Boston driving, or tame Boston drivers, in three short days. Boston is meant to be enjoyed on foot.

Boston

Boston was established in 1630, and you get a sense of its long history the moment you arrive. It is hard to walk more than a block in downtown Boston without seeing some kind of historic marker. If it weren't for the parked cars, a walk at dusk along Beacon Hill's gas-lit brick side-walks and cobblestone streets might convince you that you'd traveled back in time to the nineteenth century.

With the exception of Back Bay, a former tidal marsh area that was filled in and laid out in the mid-nineteenth century, Boston's complex network of narrow streets, distinct neighborhoods, and old brick buildings give it more the feel of a European city than of a modern American metropolis.

However, one only need look at the number of glass skyscrapers in the financial district to realize that progress has by no means passed Boston by. In addition to the thriving financial community, countless high tech firms have moved into the area during the last 15 years. Boston Harbor, once the city's mainstay, is still a busy port. Long a center of learning, Boston boasts one of the greatest concentrations of higher education institutions in the nation and is on the cutting edge of medical research. Consequently, it is an interesting, culturally diverse, and attractive city, steeped in its past yet vibrantly alive in its present.

Sightseeing Highlights

▲▲**The Boston Public Gardens**—Founded in 1897 and designed by Frederick Law Olmstead, who also created New York's Central Park, these are the oldest public gardens in the United States. The gardens are in full bloom

from April through October, but the stately trees and
beautiful landscaping make them a pleasure to visit
in any season. Children will love the "Make Way for
Ducklings" sculpture, depicting a scene from the book of
the same name, and a ride on Boston's own Swan Boats.
A swan boat ride is a relaxing way for adults to get perspective on the city as well. The boats operate from 10:00
a.m. to 4:00 p.m. mid-April through mid-June and 10:00
a.m. to 5:00 p.m. mid-June through Labor Day (weather
permitting). A small fee is charged.

▲▲▲**The Freedom Trail**—The trail is a 3-mile walking
tour of many of Boston's historical sites. It begins at the
information booth in Boston Common on Tremont Street
between the Park Street and Tremont Street subway stations. Sightseeing tours also travel the 3-mile route. You
can get tour information from the visitor information
kiosk. Though the trail is well marked by a red line on the
pavement, it is a good idea to get a trail map at the information booth in case you decide to stray from the main
route. The map also contains background information on
each site.

The first stop on the Freedom Trail is the "new" **State
House**, designed by respected architect Charles Bullfinch
and built in 1795. The Capitol was built on land belonging

to John Hancock's family, and Samuel Adams laid the cornerstone. The State House can be toured free from 10:00 a.m. to 4:00 p.m. Monday through Friday.

The next stop is the **Park Street Church** and **Granary Burying Ground** where John Hancock and Samuel Adams lie buried near victims of the Boston Massacre. A little farther down Tremont Street is **King's Chapel**, built in 1754. Behind the chapel on School Street is the **Old City Hall**, now home to a marvelous French restaurant, Maison Robert, and a commemorative statue of Benjamin Franklin. Several doors down on the corner of School and Washington streets is the **Old Corner Bookstore** in a lovely brick building that dates back to 1712. Now known for its fine selection of regional and travel titles, the store is steeped in literary history: such notable literary figures as Henry David Thoreau, Henry Wadsworth Longfellow, Ralph Waldo Emerson, and Judge Oliver Wendell Holmes met there in the 1800s to discuss topics of the day.

Diagonally across from the Old Corner Bookstore at the **Old South Meeting House**, you can view a multi-media presentation on the building's role in history: Boston Tea Party rallies were held here. The meeting house was built in 1729. Admission is $2 for adults, $1.50 for seniors and students, 75 cents for children 6 to 16. Hours are 9:30 a.m. to 5:00 p.m. daily April through October; 10:00 a.m. to 4:00 p.m. weekdays and 10:00 a.m. to 5:00 p.m. weekends during the rest of the year.

The **Old State House** at Washington and State streets is the next stop on the trail. It was built in 1712 and currently houses exhibits on Boston history. Admission to the museum is $2 for adults, $1.50 for seniors and students, 75 cents for children 6 to 18. It is open daily from 9:30 a.m. to 5:00 p.m. during the summer and on Saturday throughout the year. It opens at 10:00 a.m. and closes at 4:00 p.m. Monday through Friday, 11:00 a.m. to 5:00 p.m. on Sunday during the winter. Just outside the State House is the site of the Boston Massacre, where five colonists were slain by British soldiers in 1770, foreshadowing the Revolutionary War.

From the State House you'll pass through **Faneuil Hall** and **Quincy Market**, old buildings that have recently been refurbished to serve as a major focal point for entertainment, dining, and shopping in the city. Return this evening for a more leisurely visit.

From Quincy Market, cross under Interstate 93 to Boston's thriving Italian North End. Visit Paul Revere's home before treating yourself to a memorable lunch in one of the North End's fabulous bistros. The **Revere House**, built in 1676, is the oldest building still standing in the city of Boston. Admission to the house is $2 for adults, $1.50 for seniors and students, 75 cents for children 5 to 17. The house is open daily from 9:30 a.m. to 5:15 p.m. during the summer, from 9:30 a.m. to 4:15 p.m. during the winter. **The Pierce/Hicborn House** next door can be toured with the Revere House for a combined admission charge of $3.25 for adults, $2.25 for students and seniors, $1 for children.

After lunch, pick up the Freedom Trail again and visit the **Old North Church** where the famed lanterns ("one if by land, two if by sea") warned of the British arrival the night of Paul Revere's ride. Farther up Hull Street, you'll pass the old **Cop's Hill Burial Ground** where Edward Hartt, the builder of the USS *Constitution*, was buried. Cross the Charlestown Bridge to the Charlestown Navy Yard to view his creation, also known as "Old Ironsides." The ship was built in 1797, saw active duty in the War of 1812, and is the oldest commissioned warship afloat today. There is also a **USS *Constitution* Museum**, open year-round. Admission is charged for the museum, but the ship itself is free. Museum hours are 9:00 a.m. to 6:00 p.m. in the summer, 9:00 a.m. to 4:00 p.m. in the winter, 9:00 a.m. to 5:00 p.m. in the spring and fall. It is closed Thanksgiving, Christmas, and New Year's Day.

Just outside the entrance to the Navy Yard you can see a multimedia re-creation of the battle of Bunker Hill at **The Bunker Hill Pavilion**. Reenactments are shown every half hour, and the pavilion is open daily from 9:30 a.m. to 4:00 p.m. Admission is $3 for adults, $1.50 for children ages 5 and up, $8 for families. Then, walk up the hill to the 220-foot-tall **Bunker Hill Monument** that commemorates the major Revolutionary War battle. The monument is open from 9:30 a.m. to 6:00 p.m. June through August, from 9:30 a.m. to 4:00 p.m. September through May. Entrance to the monument is free.

As an alternative to retracing your steps to Faneuil Hall Marketplace on the Freedom Trail, MBTA buses run frequently from Charlestown to downtown Boston and the Faneuil Hall area, letting you save your energy for a stroll through the market.

Lodging

Cosmopolitan city that it is, Boston has plenty of high-class hotels to bathe you in luxury. The **Meridien** (617-451-1900 or 800-543-4300) in the financial district has one of the better restaurants in the city—**Julien's**. Doubles start at $220. The **Bostonian** (617-523-3600 or 800-343-0922), adjacent to Quincy Market and Haymarket, and a short walk from the North End, has one of the best locations in the city for sightseeing. Doubles range from $235 to $290. **The Ritz-Carlton** (617-536-5700 or 800-241-3333) overlooking the Public Gardens is where visiting heads of state stay. Double rooms average $235 to $365. The **Four Seasons** (617-338-4400 or 800-332-3442) is also adjacent to the Public Gardens, and doubles start at $160 on the weekends and run to $400 for a deluxe suite during the week. The **Copley Plaza** (617-267-5300 or 800-826-7539) has one of the most sumptuous lobbies in Boston and is conveniently located in Copley Square. Doubles range from $190 to $260 per night. **The Boston Harbor Hotel** (617-439-7000 or 800-752-7077) on the waterfront is an elegant new addition to the Boston lodging scene. Water taxis from the airport stop right at its doorstep. Double rooms with a city view start at $240, and those with a harbor view start at $290. Many of these hotels do have special weekend rates, making them a little more affordable than during the week.

The Lenox Hotel at 710 Boylston Street at Copley Square (617-536-5300 or 800-225-7676) and **The Omni Parker House** (617-227-8600 or 800-THE-OMNI), which is

on the Freedom Trail just a few blocks from Quincy
Market, are more reasonably priced than the hotels listed
above and are still convenient to sights. Doubles at the
Parker House, which tend to be on the small side, start at
$180, while rooms at the Lenox start at $155. Even more of
a bargain is the **Howard Johnson's** in Kenmore Square
(617-267-3100 or 800-654-2000). For a homier atmosphere,
try **Beacon Hill Bed & Breakfast** at 27 Brimmer Street on
the residential "flats" of Beacon Hill near the Charles River.
Rooms including breakfast go for $115 to $135 per night
(617-523-7376).

Staying in Harvard Square in Cambridge is a pleasant
alternative to staying in Boston. There is always something
happening in the square, and Boston is an easy subway ride
away. The **Charles Hotel** (617-864-1200 or 800-882-1818) is
the upscale lodging choice with doubles ranging from $139
to $239, while the **Harvard Manor House** (617-864-5200 or
800-458-5886) across the street offers comfortable motel-
style accommodations for around $100 per night. One of the
newest lodgings to grace Harvard Square is the **Inn at
Harvard** (617-491-2222 or 800-222-8733). With its elegant
atrium lounge and attractive guest rooms, the inn is both
comfortable and convenient (doubles $160 to $195).

The Boston International Hostel at 12 Hemenway
Street offers dormitory accommodations for only $14 to $17
per night. The hostel is close to the Boylston subway stop
on the Green Line, to Newbury Street, and to the
Prudential Center and only a five-minute walk from the
Museum of Fine Arts. It has a fully equipped kitchen and
showers and is handicapped accessible (617-536-9455).

For a more complete listing of hotels in the area, write
the **Massachusetts Lodging Association** at 148 State
Street, Suite 400, Boston, MA 02109. They produce a free
lodging directory. **Bed & Breakfast Agency of Boston**
(617-720-3540 or 800-CITY BNB) can help you find a bed
and breakfast in the area that's right for your needs. In
general, if you are willing to stay outside the city, you'll
probably find a wider range of inexpensive hotels. You
will not, of course, have the convenience of the city at
your doorstep.

Dining

While Boston has no shortage of good restaurants, four eateries have remained popular for more than 100 years. The **Locke Ober Cafe** (617-542-1340), down an alley off Winter Street, was established in 1875. It is an old-money institution with dark wood paneling, hard-backed leather chairs, and a men's club atmosphere. Prices are expensive. **Jacob Wirth's** (617-338-8586), across from the New England Medical Center near Chinatown, has changed little over the last century. The wooden floors are well worn, the home-brewed beer (both light and dark) is full-bodied, the hearty meals have a German flavor, and prices are moderate. **Durgin Park** (617-227-2038) in Faneuil Hall Marketplace is yet another Boston landmark, noted for New England-style meals, large portions, and surly wait-resses. The restaurant originally served the men who worked the docks (big meals at low prices) and has tried to retain the same atmosphere, although prices are no longer dirt cheap. Just around the corner, the **Union Oyster House** (617-227-2750), established in 1826, has a raw oyster bar and specializes in seafood. Entrees range from $15 to $25. The quality of the food has slipped somewhat in recent years at Locke Ober, Durgin Park, and the Union Oyster House, and the restaurants seem to be riding on their reputation a bit. However, they are still worth visiting for tradition's sake.

Anthony's Pier 4 at 140 Atlantic Avenue overlooking the harbor and Boston serves seafood on a grand scale. In size, Anthony's is more like a factory than a restaurant, and while it's standards are not what they used to be, it manages to maintain a pleasant atmosphere. Tasty dishes from the sea come with freshly baked popovers, and if you have room for dessert, the baked Alaska is sure to please. Try to get a seat outdoors in the summer. Call (617) 423-6363 for reservations. The **Boston Sail Loft** at 80 Atlantic Avenue also specializes in seafood and over-looks the water, but in a crowded yet relaxed milieu. The menu includes sandwiches, chowder, salads, and pub fare at moderate prices. About a five-minute walk from Faneuil Hall, it is a popular night spot with local young profes-

sionals. Even more casual and crowded is **No Name** in
the wharf area of the waterfront. What it lacks in ambience, No Name makes up for in low prices and the fresh-
ness of their seafood. Call (617) 338-7539 for directions
since the restaurant is hard to find, and be prepared to
wait on line. They do not take reservations. **Legal
Seafoods** in the Boston Park Plaza hotel is also known for
its seafaring cuisine (617-426-4444). **Skipjack's**, a relative
newcomer, is quickly gaining acceptance for its innovative
seafood dishes (199 Clarendon, telephone 617-536-4949).

You'll be able to get fresh fish most anywhere on this
trip. What you won't find elsewhere in New England is
the variety of excellent ethnic restaurants that Boston has
to offer. Try several of them while you're here. There are
two **King & I** restaurants in Boston, at 259 Newbury Street
(617-437-9611) and at 145 Charles Street on Beacon Hill
(617-227-3320). Both have the same menu offering delicious Thai cuisine, with dinner entrees averaging $9,
lunch entrees $5.50. The spicy aroma of **Kebab n'Kurry**,
at Massachusetts Avenue and Beacon Street, can easily
entice you into ordering more than you can possibly eat,
and everything you sample will be delectable. The basement Indian restaurant is casual and affordably priced.
Call (617)536-9835. A little bit pricier, **Casa Romero** specializes in gourmet Mexican and southwestern dishes.
The restaurant, located in the alley just off Gloucester
and Newbury streets, is open Monday through Saturday.
Reservations are recommended since the chef's talents
are renowned in the area (617-536-4341). **Jae's Cafe** on
revitalized Columbus Avenue (617-421-9405) serves delicious Korean noodle and rice dishes ranging from $6.95
to $11.95. At **Nara**, on Wendell Street deep in the heart
of the financial district (call 617-338-5935 for directions),
a wide variety of sushi selections are rolled to order. The
teriyaki dishes are also terrific. Busy during weekday
lunch hours, this cozy restaurant is refreshingly quiet
in the evenings.

The North End is the place to go for Italian cuisine.
Felicia's (617-523-9885) and **Villa Francesca** (617-367-
2948) on Richmond Street are somewhat expensive, but

the food, particularly at Francesca's, is worth its price.
La Piccola Venezia (617-523-9802) at 63 Salem Street
serves traditional Italian specialties such as cannelloni,
manicotti, veal parmigiana, and lasagna in an informal setting. The menu is written on chalkboards throughout the
tiny restaurant. Lunch or dinner for two will be in the $20
range; bring a hearty appetite as the portions are huge!
L'Osteria (617-723-7847), just down the street at 109
Salem, serves melt-in-your-mouth eggplant parmigiana, or
if you like shrimp—try the savory shrimp Francese. It is
not unusual to see a line of people waiting outside North
End restaurants on weekend nights since most do not take
reservations. If you visit Boston during the summer, you
may be lucky enough to come upon one of the neighborhood's Italian festivals. You can literally eat your way
through the streets! Call (617) 536-4100 for festival information.

Chinatown has a wide selection of Oriental restaurants,
enough so that you can walk down the street and eat at
whichever one appeals to you the most. Although I've
never had a bad meal in Chinatown, my favorite is the
Lucky Dragon at 45 Beach Street. For a spicy inexpensive lunch, two people can share a single generous portion of their Singapore noodles (617-542-0772).

Ice Cream
As cold as the region gets in the winter, oddly enough
New England has the highest per capita consumption of
ice cream in the country. New Englanders are passionate
about their ice cream! Almost every town on the itinerary
has at least one ice cream parlor. You will be able to
locate them easily by the trail of eagerly slurping patrons.
Bostonians are connoisseurs; hence a number of locally
famous rival parlors vie for business. Wherever you
decide to sample the sweet frozen dessert, you're bound
to be pleased.

Steve's, possibly the best known of the lot, has locations throughout the area, including Quincy Market and
on Massachusetts Avenue in Back Bay. Try their mix-ins.
Crushed Oreos, Heath bars, chocolate chips, and the like,

are hand-blended into fresh ice cream made the old-fashioned way. Their hot fudge sundaes are amazing. Steve Herrell, who originally founded Steve's and later sold the company, is back with his own parlor, **Herrell's**, on Dunster Street in Cambridge. **Emack & Bolio's** on upper Newbury Street also turns out a good product. For basic family-style ice cream, **Brigham's** operates several restaurants in the city. **Il Dolce Momento** on Charles Street in Beacon Hill serves a range of unique Italian gelati flavors and sorbets. This parlor also offers tasty pastries and sandwiches (such as chicken salad with artichoke hearts).

Boston Shopping

Boston shopping affords enough variety so that any visitor should be able to find what he or she is looking for. The best shopping is clustered in five different sections of the city.

Newbury Street—This handsome street in the heart of Back Bay runs from the edge of the Public Gardens to Massachusetts Avenue and is home to the city's chic boutiques and art galleries. Sumptuous shops range from the trendy to antiques and traditional favorites such as Burberry's and Laura Ashley. You can find several interesting secondhand clothing stores toward the Massachusetts Avenue end of the street. Along the way are plenty of sidewalk cafés catering to weary shoppers. Pucker Safrai Gallery, the Copley Society, and the Victor Hugo Bookshop at number 339 are among my favorite stops on Newbury Street.

Copley Place—This high-class shopping mall is an example of Boston's recent revitalization and gentrification. The Westin and Marriott hotels are at opposite ends of the mall. Tiffany's, Neiman Marcus, and Gucci's are all located here, as well as an excellent newsstand carrying a wide variety of American and continental magazines, a six-cinema movie complex that features the fine "Where's Boston" documentary film on one screen, and a Rizzoli's bookstore. Saks Fifth Avenue and Lord & Taylor are nearby at the Prudential Center.

Downtown Crossing—This is the area of Washington Street one block east of Park Street station. Though not a visually appealing place to shop, the "World Famous Filene's Basement" is worth a stop, especially for bargain hunters. Barnes and Noble operates a large bookstore here, and fast-food addicts can have their fill at either "The Corner" or the fast-food hall upstairs at Lafayette Place.

Quincy Market—The market is a good place to browse after sightseeing, since many of the stores are open until 9:00 p.m. The specialty carts adjacent to the food hall sell everything from Celtics souvenir shirts to batik sarongs.

Haymarket—This open-air fruit and vegetable market is held every Friday and Saturday alongside Interstate 93 between Quincy Market and the North End. Many of the vendors are true characters, and the market is a ritual that has remained unchanged through the years. You can get a hunk of Brie cheese for a buck, and you may want to load up on fresh fruit and nuts for the trip. Beware: some vendors display gorgeous merchandise at rock bottom prices but fill your bag with overripe fruit from the back of the pile. Make sure you pick what you want before you hand over the money. The best selection is in the morning, while the best prices are at the end of the day when the vendors try to unload their wares rather than carry them home.

Nightlife
If you're in a bar-hopping mood, the Quincy Market area is the best place to start because of the high concentration of drinking establishments there. **Lord Bunbury's** tries to capture the flavor of an English pub and draws a young, boisterous crowd. **Houlihan's** is primarily a restaurant but has a dance floor that packs them in after dinner. **Cricket's** attracts the business-suit set, and **Lily's** has a piano bar and outdoor seating and is a great place to people-watch on hot summer nights. Near Faneuil Hall, **The Black Rose** is a lively Irish pub and *the* place to go on St. Patrick's Day, if you can get in.

Back Bay has a number of popular night spots including
Friday's on Newbury Street which has a fun menu, tasty
appetizers, and a crowded bar area in which to mix and
mingle. **Daisy Buchanan's**, also on Newbury Street, used
to be a Red Sox hangout but is now dominated by swing-
ing singles. **The Elliot Lounge**, on Massachusetts and
Commonwealth avenues, sports a relaxed and casual
atmosphere. This is where the runners flock after complet-
ing the Boston Marathon. **The Top of the Hub** atop the
Prudential building has a terrific view of the city. The
drinks aren't cheap, but the view is worth it. If your tastes
run to Broadway show tunes, try **Diamond Jim's** piano
bar at the Lenox Hotel. Patrons are welcome to stand up
and try their hand at a song or two.

On Beacon Hill one of my favorites is **The Seven's Pub**
at 77 Charles Street. They serve great sandwiches with
homemade potato salad at rock bottom prices and have a
good selection of imported beer. The milieu is smoky and
very casual. The clientele is mixed but always friendly.
Hidden away on lower Chestnut Street (#75) is the
Charles Restaurant, a classy establishment with an inti-
mate bar. Several blocks away on Beacon Street,
The Bull n' Finch Pub inspired the TV sitcom "Cheers."
Although it has lost some of its neighborhood appeal to
fame, it is still a fun place to go, especially if you are a fan
of the show. For more elegant sipping, try upstairs in the
lounge at **The Hampshire House**.

Landsdowne Street, across from Fenway Park, is lined
with nightclubs that generally cater to a young crowd,
one of the most popular being **Venus de Milo**.

Other
If a foreigner walks up to you on the streets of Boston
and asks you "where is this place that you have war," they
are probably not referring to the Bunker Hill area but to
an area known locally as the "Combat Zone." The Zone
lies between the theater district and Chinatown and is
comparable to New York City's Times Square district.
Although the Zone is shrinking, what remains is a strip
of X-rated movie houses and is best avoided.

The Performing Arts

Music lovers should not miss the world-famous **Boston Pops** or the **Boston Symphony Orchestra's** more traditional classical performances. Both make their home in Symphony Hall, except during the summer when the BSO travels to Tanglewood and the Pops give their annual Fourth of July concert at the Esplanade on the Charles River. Call (617) 266-1492 for ticket information. Boston also has its own ballet company, the **Boston Ballet**. Call (617) 695-6950 for their schedule. Annual performances of *The Nutcracker* are a holiday favorite.

The **BOSTIX** booth in Faneuil Hall Marketplace sells tickets for all major theatrical productions. Check with them to see what's in town during your visit. It is sometimes possible to get reduced ticket prices there the day of performance. Call (617) 723-5181 for up-to-date schedule and ticket information.

Sports

If you enjoy a good game of baseball, you'll especially appreciate watching one in **Fenway Park**, home of the **Boston Red Sox**. The ballpark's relatively small size makes attending a game more a participatory than a spectator sport. Call (617) 267-8661 for schedule and ticket information.

Wintertime visitors can catch either the **Boston Celtics** or **Boston Bruins** at the **Boston Garden**. Call (617) 227-3200 for the Garden's schedule and ticket information.

Racing buffs will be drawn to **Suffolk Downs** for horse racing and **Wonderland** for dog racing. Both tracks have their own stops on the Blue Line subway.

BOSTON'S MUSEUMS

The scope of Boston's museums is tremendous, from ancient Egyptian art to state-of-the-art computers, from an authentic Japanese house to lightning demonstrations, and from dolphins to European tapestries. Today you'll have a chance to uncover past civilizations and look into our own future.

Suggested Schedule

8:30 a.m.	Breakfast.
9:30 a.m.	Spend the morning exploring your choice of museums along the waterfront.
12:30 p.m.	Lunch in Chinatown.
1:30 p.m.	Visit the Boston Museum of Fine Arts.
4:00 p.m.	Visit the Isabella Stewart Gardner Museum.
Sunset	After dinner in Back Bay, visit the John Hancock Observation Deck or the Prudential's Skywalk to watch the sun set.

Sightseeing Highlights
▲**Boston Tea Party Ship & Museum**—You get to throw a tea chest overboard in protest of the British tax on this replica of the eighteenth-century ship where the famous revolt originally took place. (The chests aren't actually filled with tea and are connected by rope, but at least you get to feel like a rebel.) The museum is open daily from 9:00 a.m. to dusk except for Thanksgiving, Christmas, and New Year's Day. It is located at 300 Congress Street on Museum Wharf, and admission is charged.

▲**Boston Children's Museum (▲▲▲** If you are traveling with children)—The museum is known for its "hands-on" exhibits, Native American collection, and Japanese home painstakingly moved here piece by piece from Kyoto. Children magically become hushed when they enter the Japanese house, but in the rest of the museum laughter prevails as they try on clothes in Grandmother's

Downtown Boston

Attic, scramble up and down over several levels in the climbing structure, and blow bubbles as big as they are. Teens will enjoy "faultless jamming," in the clubhouse designed especially for them, with electronic musical instruments that sound good together no matter how they are played. The museum is open daily from 10:00 a.m. to 5:00 p.m., Friday evening until 9:00 p.m., and is closed Monday from Labor Day through June. Admission is $6 for adults, $5 for seniors and children ages 2 to 15, $2 for one-year-olds. Admission Friday evenings from 5:00 p.m. to 9:00 p.m. is only $1 for everyone. The museum is located on Congress Street at Museum Wharf. Closed New Year's, Thanksgiving, and Christmas.

▲▲**The Computer Museum**—With the influence of the high-tech industry in Boston and nearby Massachusetts Institute of Technology turning out computer geniuses of the future, it is no wonder that Boston has the first museum devoted to the history of the computer. Get a close-up look at the first computers, then test your skills

in the PC gallery. On Museum Wharf next to the
Children's Museum, the Computer Museum is open daily
10:00 a.m. to 6:00 p.m., Friday evening until 9:00 p.m.;
closed on Monday September through June. Admission is
$6 for adults, $5 for students and seniors, children under
6 free. Admission is half-price on Friday evenings.

▲▲**New England Aquarium**—What trip to the coast
would be complete without a look at the inhabitants of
the sea? The aquarium has a magnificent cylindrical glass
tank several stories high. You can view hundreds of
species of sea life including sharks, barracudas, and giant
sea turtles as you wind down the spiral ramp. Dolphin
shows are included in your admission. If you don't have
time to go in the museum, at least take a few minutes to
watch the seals play at the outside entrance to the aquarium as you stroll along the waterfront. Hours vary
depending upon the season, but the aquarium is generally
open daily from 9:00 a.m. to at least 5:00 p.m., later in the
summer. Call (617) 973-5200 for current hours during your
visit. The aquarium is located on Central Wharf, three
blocks from Faneuil Hall Marketplace next to the
Aquarium "T" stop on the Blue Line. Admission is $7.50
for adults, $6.50 for seniors, and $3.50 for children 3 to 11.

▲▲**Boston Museum of Science**—Test your strength,
then discover the power of electricity. Learn about the
earth's gravitational force, then explore faraway planets in
the planetarium. One can spend hours in this fascinating
museum unearthing the secrets of nature's unseen energy
sources, as well as those that are visible to the naked eye,
and see how man tries to tame and control them. Many of
the exhibits are participatory. The museum is open from
9:00 a.m. to 5:00 p.m. Tuesday through Sunday, and
Friday evening until 9:00 p.m. Admission is $6.50 for
adults, $4.50 for children ages 4 to 14 and for seniors.
Admission to the planetarium and Omni Theater is separate, but combination tickets are available. The museum
has its own subway stop on the Lechmere branch of the
Green Line.

▲▲▲**Boston Museum of Fine Arts**—This is one of the
most highly respected art museums in the country. The

collection consists of ancient Greek, Roman, Egyptian, and
Oriental art, with classic European and American artists
represented as well. There are also American period
rooms, early American furniture, silver, and fine musical
instruments. The West Wing addition, designed by I. M.
Pei, houses changing exhibits, an attractive restaurant, and
a superlative museum gift shop. Courtyard dining adjoins
the lower-level cafeteria. The museum is open Tuesday
through Sunday 10:00 a.m. to 5:00 p.m., Wednesday until
10:00 p.m. The West Wing is open until 10:00 p.m. on
Thursday and Friday evenings. Admission is $6 for adults,
$5 for seniors and students, $3 for children 6 to 17.
Everyone is admitted free of charge on Wednesday from
4:00 p.m. to 6:00 p.m. The museum is located on
Huntington Avenue across from Northeastern University.
The Huntington Avenue branch of the Green Line stops
right in front of the museum.

▲▲**Isabella Stewart Gardner Museum**—My favorite
museum in Boston, this Venetian-style palazzo on the
Fenway just two blocks from the Museum of Fine Arts
houses Ms. Gardner's extraordinary private collection.
Imagine having a chapel in your home with a thirteenth-
century stained-glass window and living with not one but
three Rembrandts. Ms. Gardner, an avid patron of the arts,
made it her life's work to amass this collection ranging
from early Italian religious paintings to American and
French impressionists of the last century to beautifully
intricate European laces. The courtyard, complete with
Roman statues and mosaics, is abloom with flowers in
every season and makes a splendid haven from the outside world. Concerts are given frequently in one of the
halls, usually on Sunday afternoons at 3:00 p.m. There is
also a café on the premises. Despite the much-publicized
theft of some of the museum's most famous works in
1990, it remains a treasure well worth unearthing. The
museum is open Tuesday through Sunday noon to 5:00
p.m. Admission is $6 for adults, $3 for students and senior
citizens, and children under 12 are admitted free.

▲▲**The John Hancock Observatory** or **The Skywalk
at the Prudential Building**—From the top of the John

Hancock Tower in Copley Square, or the Prudential building nearby, you'll see magnificent views of the city and
beyond on clear days and the city sparkling as night falls.
The Hancock Observatory is open Monday through
Saturday 9:00 a.m. to 11:00 p.m., Sunday from 10:00 a.m.
to 11:00 p.m., May through October, and noon to 11:00
p.m. November through April (last entry 10:15 p.m.).
Admission is $2.75 for adults, $2.00 for seniors and children 5 to 15. The Skywalk at the Prudential building just
down the street is not as tall but has views in all directions
(the Hancock is closed off on one side). Admission is
$2.75 for adults and $1.75 for seniors and children 5 to 15.

Other Sights
You may wish to seek out any of a number of small
museums that cater to special interests. The **Institute of
Contemporary Art** at 955 Boylston Street features changing exhibits of contemporary art. The museum is open
Wednesday through Sunday from 11:00 a.m. to 5:00 p.m.
and until 8:00 p.m. on Thursday and Friday evenings.
Admission is $4 for adults, $3 for students, and $1.50 for
children and seniors. The **Museum of Afro-American
Artists** focuses on visual arts. It is located at 300 Walnut
Avenue and is generally open Tuesday through Saturday
from 1:00 p.m. to 5:00 p.m., but hours can vary, so call
ahead for information (617-442-8614). Admission is $1.25
for adults, 50 cents for students and seniors. The **Christian Science Center** behind the Prudential building
is architecturally interesting, as is the **Boston Public
Library** several blocks away in Copley Square. The library
was designed by the highly regarded architectural firm
of McKim, Mead & White. Another library, the **Boston
Athenaeum** at 10½ Beacon Street near the State House, is
a long-standing Boston institution. The library's collection
includes early American publications and an exhibit
gallery of American art.
    The **Black Heritage Trail** is similar to the Freedom
Trail and highlights significant places in Boston's black
history. The **African Meeting House**, the oldest standing
black church in the United States, is one of the stops on
the trail. The main visitor center is located at 46 Joy Street,

but you can also pick up a trail brochure at the tourist information center on Boston Common. For an outdoor excursion, a visit to the **Arnold Arboretum** at the Arborway in Jamaica Plain, Boston, is well worthwhile—especially during lilac season. The 265-acre landscaped Arboretum has over 7,000 varieties of trees, and boasts the second largest collection of lilacs in all of North America with over 400 varieties. The visitor center is open from 10:00 a.m. to 4:00 p.m., the grounds from sunrise to sunset (617-524-1718).

Boston has a number of historic homes that can be toured, including the Victorian **Gibson House Museum** at 137 Beacon Street in Back Bay. (Tours are given at 2:00, 3:00, and 4:00 p.m. Wednesday through Sunday, May through October, and November through April on Saturday and Sunday by appointment; call (617) 267-6338; admission is $3). **Nichols House Museum**, an 1809 period home that once belonged to Rose Standish Nichols, is on Mt. Vernon Street atop Beacon Hill. It is open during the summer Tuesday through Saturday from 1:00 p.m. to 5:00 p.m.; and admission is $3. Hours are more limited during the rest of the year, so call (617) 267-6338 if you are interested in visiting during the off-season.

Beer lovers may wish to tour one of Boston's breweries. The **Boston Beer Company** brews local favorite Samuel Adams Lager and can be toured on Thursday and Saturday at 2:00 p.m. (617-522-9080). The **Massachusetts Bay Brewing Company** also runs brewery tours on Tuesday, Friday, and Saturday. Call (617) 574-9551 for information.

Schedule Option

Too many museums for your taste? How about a morning or afternoon harbor cruise? Most of the cruises leave from piers near the Aquarium stop on the Blue Line. The cost depends upon whether you plan to take a short cruise in the harbor or out to the harbor islands (usually only several dollars per person) or if you wish to take one on which dinner or live band music is included. Call **Bay State Cruises**, (617) 723-7800, **Boston Harbor Cruises**, (617) 227-4321, or **Massachusetts Bay Lines**, (617) 542-8000, for additional information.

Itinerary Option
If your time in the Boston area permits, modify this itinerary to add a day trip to one of New England's foremost
attractions, **Old Sturbridge Village**, a living museum that
re-creates everyday life in an 1830s New England village.
Candle making, blacksmithing, and woodworking are
among the craft demonstrations you'll see there. Although
children especially enjoy the village, adults will certainly
be impressed as well. The village is open year-round
(10:00 a.m. to 4:00 p.m. during the winter; 9:00 a.m. to
5:00 p.m. the rest of the year), except for major holidays
and Mondays during the winter months. Admission is
high—$14 for adults, $7 for children 6 to 15—but the visit
is an all-day event. From Boston, take the Massachusetts
Turnpike (Interstate 90) west to Exit 9 and follow signs
to the village.

The Sturbridge area is also one of the largest apple
growing regions in the state, and many of the orchards
have "pick your own" programs, making a Sturbridge outing fun for the whole family, especially on a crisp, clear
autumn day. The trip from Boston is about 60 miles each
way. If you want to spend the night in Sturbridge, the
Publick House & Country Motor Lodge is a popular
spot. Call (508) 347-3313 or 800-PUBLICK for reservations.

CAMBRIDGE

Cambridge, like Boston, has been around for over 350 years. Remarkably, Harvard University has been in existence almost as long, and its influence is felt in just about every aspect of Cambridge life, particularly in bustling Harvard Square.

Suggested Schedule

9:00 a.m.	Travel from Boston to Cambridge.
9:30 a.m.	Spend the morning on the grounds and in the museums of the nation's oldest university, Harvard.
12:00 noon	Lunch.
1:00 p.m.	Walk down Brattle Street as far as Fresh Pond Parkway to view Cambridge's loveliest homes. Visit the home of Henry Wadsworth Longfellow on the return trip.
3:00 p.m.	Spend the rest of the afternoon browsing through Harvard Square's many bookshops and boutiques.
6:00 p.m.	Dinner in Cambridge, then visit an area nightclub.

Travel Route
If you're coming from downtown Boston, take the Red Line on the subway toward Alewife and get off at the Harvard Square stop.

Sightseeing Highlights
▲▲▲**Harvard University**—This is the oldest university in the United States. Its ivy-covered buildings and quiet courtyards (in some areas of the school) make it one of the prettiest as well. Stop in at Widener Library as you walk through "The Yard"; it has one of the most extensive collections of any library in the country. The library has a small exhibit depicting Cambridge history which may help put the city in perspective.

Harvard's huge endowment has given the school outstanding museums and innumerable buildings of interest.
See if you can guess which one was funded by a major
camera company (hint: it's near The Yard). The **Fogg Art
Museum** (32 Quincy St.), with its fine collection of
impressionist works, including a Degas ballerina, and
Romanesque and medieval works, is my favorite Harvard
museum. At the **Busch Reisinger** (29 Kirkland St.), the
specialty is German expressionism. The **Sackler** (Quincy
St. and Broadway), the newest of the Harvard museums,
concentrates on Far Eastern and Islamic works of art. One
admission charge of $4 for adults, $2.50 for students and
seniors (children are free), covers all three museums.
They are open Tuesday through Sunday 10:00 a.m. to
5:00 p.m. and are free to all visitors on Saturdays from
10:00 a.m. to 12:00 p.m.

Also operated by Harvard are the **Botanical Museum**
with its unusual glass flowers exhibit, the **Peabody
Museum of Archaeology and Ethnology**, the **Museum
of Comparative Zoology**, the **Mineralogical and
Geological Museum**, and the **Semitic Museum**. These
museums are located on Oxford Street and Divinity
Avenue. The Semitic Museum is open Monday through
Friday 11:00 a.m. to 5:00 p.m., Sunday 1:00 p.m. to 5:00
p.m. The others (all housed in the same building) are
open Monday through Saturday 9:00 a.m. to 4:30 p.m.,
Sunday from 1:00 p.m. to 4:15 p.m.; admission is $4 for
adults, $3 for seniors and students, $1 for children 3 to
13. The museums are closed on major holidays. Call (617)
495-1910 for additional information.

▲▲**Longfellow National Historic Site**—This was the
home of poet Henry Wadsworth Longfellow for 45 years
until his death in 1882. His major works were written
here, among them *Hiawatha* and *Evangeline*. The house,
built in 1759, has additional historic significance as
George Washington's headquarters during the siege of
Boston in 1776. It is open daily from 10:00 a.m. to 4:30
p.m. except for Thanksgiving, Christmas, and New Year's
Day, and is just one of many beautiful homes along
Brattle Street. Admission is $2. There is no charge for
seniors and children under 16.

▲**MIT Museum**—In addition to exhibits on holography, engineering, science, and architecture—exhibits you'd expect from a university that has produced some of the world's greatest scientific minds—this museum also has an art collection and a model ship gallery. The main museum is located at 265 Massachusetts Avenue near Central Square and is open Tuesday through Friday from 9:00 a.m. to 5:00 p.m. and on weekends from 1:00 p.m. to 5:00 p.m. Admission is $2 for adults. The Compton Gallery is in building 10 of the school's main campus (open Monday through Friday 9:00 a.m. to 5:00 p.m.), and the Hart Nautical Galleries are in building 5 (open daily 9:00 a.m. to 8:00 p.m.).

▲**Mount Auburn Cemetery**—This is one of the most beautifully landscaped urban cemeteries anywhere. There's even a small lookout tower where you can view the surrounding cities of Cambridge and Boston. Charles Bullfinch (the architect who designed the State House), American artist Winslow Homer, Henry Wadsworth Longfellow, and Oliver Wendell Holmes are all buried here. At 580 Mt. Auburn Street, it is a bit of a walk from Harvard Square but may be worthwhile if you appreciate historic tombstones.

Helpful Hints

The Cambridge Discovery Booth next to the "T" station in Harvard Square sells historic walking tour maps of the area for $1. The booth is open 9:00 a.m. to 5:00 p.m. Monday through Saturday, 1:00 p.m. to 5:00 p.m. on Sunday mid-June through Labor Day, on weekends only through October. Call (617) 497-1630 for information.

Cambridge Shopping

Because of its proximity to Harvard University, Harvard Square has more than its share of bookstores. **The Coop** (Harvard Cooperative Society), Harvard University's main bookstore, also has considerable record and art print departments. **Wordsworth** and the **Harvard Square Bookstore** are two bookstores where you can browse to your heart's content, since both are open late. When you run out of bookstores, there are plenty of clothing stores and specialty shops, particularly in the **Galleria** and **Charles Hotel** shopping complexes, to keep even the most determined shopper busy for hours. Don't miss the newsstand in the center of Harvard Square: its selection of magazines and newspapers seems endless.

Dining

Harvard Square's restaurants run the gamut from fast-food establishments to upscale bistros. **The Wursthaus** on JFK Street serves excellent lox, bagels, and cream cheese, cold-cut platters, and a marvelous selection of beers from around the world. Try **Yenching** (617-547-1130) on Massachusetts Avenue near the "T" station for good Chinese food at moderate prices. **Au Bon Pain**, next to Yenching, is the place to people-watch at outdoor tables. Study chess players intent on their game as you sample croissants in every flavor imaginable, gourmet sandwiches such as tarragon chicken or chicken with bernaise, and creamy soups from Au Bon Pain's kitchen for as little as $3.50 per meal. **Grendel's Den** (617-491-1050), at JFK and Winthrop streets, has a terrific salad bar, good Greek combo plates, and a pleasant atmosphere. Prices start around $6.

The Garage on the corner of Mt. Auburn, JFK, and Dunster streets is filled with out-of-the-ordinary fast-food restaurants. **Formaggio's** creates unique sandwiches with fillings such as ratatouille and boursin cheese on fresh homemade bread. At **Baby Watson's**, chocoholics must try the "chocolate orgasms"; the cheesecake is also pretty irresistible. **Cafe Aventura** serves great pizza for a song. **Leo's Place**, across the street from the Garage, offers the best basic Swiss burger and fries around.

At the other end of the spectrum is **Upstairs at the Pudding** (617-864-1933) for fine dining. The "Pudding" is at 10 Holyoke Street, reservations are recommended, and meals are expensive. At the **Averof** (617-354-4500) in Porter Square belly dancers perform while patrons dine on Greek specialties.

Nightlife

Ryles Jazz Club in Inman Square has long been recognized as one of the Boston area's best jazz bars (617-876-9330). The **Regattabar** at the Charles Hotel in Harvard Square also has live jazz most evenings. Blues musicians perform nightly at actor Dan Ackroyd's **House of Blues** at 96 Winthrop Street (617-491-2583). The cover charge varies, and there's a gospel brunch on Sundays. The **Brattle Theatre** (617-876-6837) on Brattle Street in Harvard Square shows current art films, revives old film classics, and occasionally runs film festivals.

CONCORD AND LEXINGTON

The first shot in the Revolutionary War was fired in Concord on April 19, 1775. During the hundred years that followed, Concord was also home to some of America's foremost literary figures—Ralph Waldo Emerson, Nathaniel Hawthorne, Louisa May Alcott, and Henry David Thoreau. As a result of Thoreau's strong naturalist influence, parts of Concord have been set aside as nature preserves. Today you'll see what inspired writers to live in Concord. Then visit neighboring Lexington, which also has its share of charm and history.

Suggested Schedule

8:00 a.m.	Breakfast.
8:30 a.m.	Leave for Concord.
9:00 a.m.	Visit the historic North Bridge, Sleepy Hollow Cemetery, and Great Meadows Wildlife Refuge.
11:00 a.m.	Tour the Concord Museum.
12:00 noon	Drive to Walden Pond for a midday hike, swim, and picnic lunch.
2:00 p.m.	Visit the Old Manse, Orchard House, Emerson's House, or the Thoreau Lyceum.
3:00 p.m.	Travel to Lexington to visit the Museum of Our National Heritage.
4:30 p.m.	Leave for Salem.
5:30 p.m.	Check into accommodations.

Travel Route: Boston to Concord to Salem (60 miles)
From Boston, take Storrow Drive west following signs to Fresh Pond Parkway and Arlington. Get on Fresh Pond Parkway and follow signs to Route 2. The entrance to Route 2 is two-thirds of the way around the second rotary.

If this is your first experience with rotaries, a word of caution: these circular intersections often found in Massachusetts when three or more roads come together can be dangerous, so approach them carefully. A

Massachusetts driver's approach to rotaries is, "Close your eyes and go." While this is not recommended, neither is timidity. Many unaccustomed drivers get hit because they hesitate too long. Try to blend into rotary traffic as easily as possible, moving at a slow but steady speed. Do not stop in the middle of a rotary! If you miss your exit, just continue on around and exit on your next circuit.

Once on Route 2 west, it's about a 15-minute drive to Concord. Follow signs to Concord center. There is a tourist information booth on your left as you approach the center.

From Concord, take Route 2A east to Lexington. You will cross Interstate 95/Route 128 before reaching the Museum of Our National Heritage. You may want to pick up fresh fruit for the trip at one of the roadside farm stands along the route.

From Lexington, take Interstate 95/Route 128 north toward Gloucester. I-95 splits off from Route 128 at Wakefield. Stay on Route 128 to Exit 35E, Route 114 east for Salem. The Lexington and Salem exits are approximately 20 miles apart. Should you wish to stay in Marblehead for the night, continue on Route 114 east from Salem for 5 miles, then follow signs to Marblehead Center.

Sightseeing Highlights

▲▲▲**The North Bridge**—On this site, British and Revolutionary troops first clashed. Visit the bridge more for its historical significance than for what you'll see here today. The Minute Man statue now stands at the site in memory of that fateful battle. The statue was sculpted by Daniel Chester French, whose grave is in nearby Sleepy Hollow Cemetery and whose home and studio you'll visit later in the trip. The visitor center on the hill above the bridge houses a gift shop and replicas of military attire that the minutemen used. The bridge is on Monument Street about ¾-mile from the center of Concord. There is no admission fee to the site, but admission is charged if you wish to visit the visitor center.

▲**Sleepy Hollow Cemetery**—As you travel back toward Concord center from the North Bridge, turn left onto

Concord and Lexington

Bedford Street. The entrance to the cemetery will be on
your left. Follow signs to Author's Ridge. Ralph Waldo
Emerson, Henry David Thoreau, Nathaniel Hawthorne,
Louisa May Alcott, and sculptor Daniel Chester French are
all buried here.

▲**Great Meadows Wildlife Refuge**—This marshy area
was frequented by Thoreau in his study of nature. Today
you can follow the 1¾-mile Dike Trail loop and perhaps
see a fox, muskrat, or weasel in addition to the various
species of waterfowl that nest in the wetlands. To get
there from the cemetery, continue on Bedford Road for
about three-fourths of a mile, then turn left onto Monsen
Road. Stay on Monsen Road to the refuge entrance.

▲▲**Concord Museum**—The museum brings together
Concord's military and literary histories. Items of interest
on the museum tour include Paul Revere's lantern, which
hung in the Old North Church in Boston the night of his
famous ride, and personal articles of Henry David
Thoreau and Ralph Waldo Emerson, who were friends as
well as fellow writers. The museum is open from 10:00
a.m. to 5:00 p.m. Tuesday through Saturday, from 1:00
p.m. to 5:00 p.m. Sunday. It is closed on major holidays.
Admission is $5 for adults, $4 for seniors and students,
$1.50 for children. The museum is at 200 Lexington Road,
just east of the intersection of Routes 2 and 2A.

▲**Walden Pond**—Henry David Thoreau's famous retreat from "civilization" is now a popular escape for Boston city dwellers and their suburban counterparts. Being relatively mud-free compared to most ponds, and much warmer than the Atlantic, Walden Pond is a preferred place to swim in the area. The pond can get crowded on a hot summer day, but the farther you walk from the main beach, the better chance you have of finding a secluded pond-side picnic spot. There is a model of Thoreau's house next to the parking lot, and the actual house site is about a ten-minute walk in from Route 126. There is a charge for the parking lot, and it is the only legal spot to park within walking distance. To get to the pond, follow Walden Street from Concord center south for about a mile. You will cross Route 2, and the pond will be on your right, the parking lot on your left.

▲**The Old Manse**—On Monument Street just below the North Bridge, the Old Manse was built in 1770 and was, at different times, home to both Emerson and Nathaniel Hawthorne. The house is open seasonally. Call (508) 369-3909 for hours of operation. Admission is $4 for adults, $2.50 for senior citizens, $1.50 for children 6 to 16.

▲**Orchard House**—This was the home of Louisa May Alcott from 1858 to 1877 and the setting for her famous novel, *Little Women*. Many actual furnishings are on display, including sketches done by an Alcott sister which still remain on one of the bedroom walls. The chapel in back of the house was built in 1884 to house meetings of the Concord School of Philosophy. The school was founded by A. Bronson Alcott, Louisa's father. The house is open for tours April through October 10:00 a.m. to 4:30 p.m. Monday through Saturday, Sundays and holidays from 1:00 p.m. to 4:30 p.m. Admission is $4 for adults, $3.50 for senior citizens and students 13 to 18, $2.50 for children 6 to 12. The house is on Route 2A (Lexington Road) going toward Lexington. Call (508) 369-4118 for winter hours.

▲**Emerson's House**—Ralph Waldo Emerson lived here for almost 50 years until his death in 1882. Many of the writer's personal artifacts are on display, including a desk he used and part of his personal library. On Cambridge Turnpike just across from the Concord Museum, the house is open from mid-April through mid-October, Thursday through Saturday from 10:00 a.m. to 4:30 p.m., Sunday from 2:00 p.m. to 4:30 p.m. Admission is $3.50 for adults and $2 for children 6-17.

▲**Thoreau Lyceum**—At 156 Belknap Street, the Lyceum is filled with Thoreau memorabilia and includes a bookshop and library specializing in Thoreau's works and a replica of his house at Walden Pond. The Lyceum is open from 10:00 a.m. to 5:00 p.m. Monday through Saturday, 2:00 p.m. to 5:00 p.m. on Sunday. It is closed major holidays. Admission is $2 for adults, $1.50 for students, 50 cents for children under 12.

▲**The Wayside**—Louisa May Alcott and Nathaniel Hawthorne both lived in this nineteenth-century home. The house is open seasonally, and admission is charged. Call (508) 369-6975 for hours it is open during your visit.

▲**Museum of Our National Heritage**—The museum is devoted to preserving and showing virtually all facets of America's heritage through changing exhibits that range from antique quilts to decorative arts to early military paraphernalia. It is open year-round, Monday through Saturday 10:00 a.m. to 5:00 p.m., Sunday noon to 5:00 p.m., closing only for Thanksgiving, Christmas, and New Year's Day. Admission is free. The museum is located at 33 Marrett Road on Route 2A in Lexington.

Lodging

In Salem, the following inn establishments are all close to the main tourist attractions. **The Salem Inn** at 7 Summer Street is in an attractive old brick building, diagonally across from the Witch House. Double rooms start at $95, and jacuzzi suites run $125 (508-741-0680 or 800-446-2995). The **Hawthorne Hotel**, an elegant small hotel on the town common, keeps company with Salem's stateliest homes. Doubles start at $92 per night (508-744-4080 or 800-SAY-STAY). The **Stepping Stone Inn** (508-741-8900 or 800-338-3022), adjacent to the Witch Museum at 19 Washington Square, is a cozy bed and breakfast with a cheery breakfast room and central location ($65-$95 including continental breakfast). The Salem Inn and Hawthorne Hotel both have decent restaurants as well.

Although you will be spending a full day exploring Salem tomorrow, and the accommodations listed above are convenient to sights, you may wish to travel 6 miles farther to the charming seaside town of Marblehead for lodging tonight and tomorrow night. A stroll down its winding streets, a seafood dinner overlooking the water, and a drive out onto affluent Marblehead Neck are all excellent ways to relax after a busy day of sightseeing. Two bed and breakfasts that overlook the ocean are **Spray Cliff** (make reservations through the Salem Inn, 508-741-0680) at 25 Spray Avenue and **Harborside House** (617-631-1032) at 23 Gregory Street. Both offer continental breakfast but only a few rooms, so reservations are wise. Rooms run from $105 to $200 at the Spray Cliff, and $65 to $85 at Harborside House. **10 Mugford Street** is also a pleasant bed and breakfast that serves a buffet-style breakfast in the morning. A two-room suite with a private bath is $95. Call (617) 639-0343 for reservations.

Camping
There are campsites at **Winter Island Maritime Park** at 50 Winter Island Road in Salem. Sites are $15 to $18, and the campground is open May through October. A trolley stops at the campground and will take you to Salem's historic sights. Call (508) 745-9430 for information.

Dining
In Salem, **Pickering Wharf** has the highest concentration of restaurants, generally fast-food and take-out operations ranging from Chinese to pizza. **Victoria Station** (508-745-3400), at Pickering Wharf on the water, has outdoor seating in summer and good steak and seafood dinner entrées that run from $10.95 to $16.95. Lunch prices start around $5. The **Chase Restaurant** (508-744-0000), also at Pickering Wharf, is a popular Salem dining spot.

In Marblehead, **Rosalie's** at 18 Sewall Street is the place to go. Rosalie's delicious northern Italian cuisine is generally considered to be the best Italian food north of Boston. Entrées range in price from the low to high teens, and reservations are a must (617-631-5353). **Danielle's Café** downstairs, named for Rosalie's daughter, serves northern Italian cuisine in a festive setting. All entrées are under $10. **The Barnacle** (617-631-4236) and **The Landing** (617-631-1878) both overlook Marblehead harbor and serve fresh seafood. Prices are moderate to expensive. **The King's Rook** at 12 State Street is a cozy coffeehouse that serves copious salads and tasty desserts (617-631-9838). Chocolate lovers must find their way to **Stowaway Sweets** candy shop at 154 Atlantic Avenue. The "chocolate meltaways" are positively out of this world (617-631-0303).

SALEM

Salem is both beguiling and bewitching. It is a small city struggling to preserve its past glory while striving to keep pace with the twentieth century. The infamous witch trials of 1692 took place in Salem, and the House of Seven Gables immortalized by Hawthorne is here. Fewer people know about Salem's prominence in early America's foreign trade network. Today we'll examine all three facets of Salem's past.

Suggested Schedule

9:00 a.m.	Breakfast, then stroll past beautiful Federalist homes on Washington Square surrounding the Salem Common.
10:00 a.m.	Visit the Salem Witch Museum.
11:00 a.m.	Visit the Peabody Museum.
1:00 p.m.	Lunch.
2:00 p.m.	Spend mid-afternoon touring Essex Institute, the Witch House, a historic home, or just window-shopping.
4:00 p.m.	End your day in Salem with a visit to the House of Seven Gables.

Travel Route

Most of the day will be spent on foot. Use caution when driving in Salem's center. There is at least one intersection where as many as six roads come together without so much as a stoplight, stop sign, or yield sign. The last time I was there, the most courteous driver in the intersection was a taxi driver.

Sightseeing Highlights

Salem—In 1692, mass hysteria gripped the city of Salem when several girls were said to have been bewitched by a West Indian servant named Tituba. This started a rash of accusations, and just about anyone exhibiting strange behavior was said to be a witch. More than two hundred

Salem

townsfolk in all were arrested for allegedly practicing witchcraft. Nineteen of the accused were hung before Massachusetts Governor William Phipps put a stop to the executions
in 1693. However, the events of 1692 were so traumatic
that Salem is known, even today, as the "witch city."

▲▲**The Salem Witch Museum**—On Salem Common, the
museum houses an audiovisual presentation of the events
of 1692. It is an engaging introduction to the history of the
witch trials. The museum is open daily from 10:00 a.m. to
5:00 p.m., to 7:00 p.m. during July and August. Admission
is $4 for adults, $3.50 for seniors, and $2.50 for students
and children 6 to 14. The presentation is shown on the
hour and half hour.

▲**The Witch House**—On the corner of Essex and
Washington streets, this building is known as the witch
house because those accused of being witches were inter-
rogated here by Judge Jonathan Corwin before going to
trial. Built around 1642, it is one of the oldest houses still
standing in the United States. Tour guides explain uses of
eighteenth-century everyday household items and how

expressions such as "sleep tight" and "turning the tables" originally came into our language. Admission is $3 for adults, $1.50 for children 5 to 16. The house is open seasonally from mid-March through November 10:00 a.m. to 4:30 p.m., to 6:00 p.m. during July and August.

▲**The Witches Dungeon**—The trial of Sarah Goode, one of the accused witches, is reenacted at 16 Lynde Street in a re-creation of the dungeon where alleged witches awaited hanging. Open daily from 10:00 a.m. to 5:00 p.m. May through November. Admission is $3.50 for adults, $2 for children 6 to 14.

▲▲**Essex Institute**—At 132 Essex Street, the institute consists of a museum building containing a collection of art, silver, dolls, toys, and military artifacts from Essex County and four period homes, the oldest dating from 1684. The institute operates special witchcraft and Salem history tours during the summer. The last tour of the day leaves at 3:30 p.m. The museum is open Monday through Saturday 10:00 a.m. to 5:00 p.m., Sundays and holidays 12:00 to 5:00 p.m.; closed Mondays December through April. The admission charge varies depending on whether you visit only the museum or also tour one or more of the historic houses.

▲▲▲**The Peabody Museum**—On East India Square at Liberty and Essex streets, the Peabody is a gem, with extraordinary depth for a small city museum. There are exhibits of nautical paintings and instruments and ships' figureheads, as one might expect in a city whose livelihood came from the sea. However, the most fascinating exhibits are those devoted to goods brought back to this country through foreign trade. The collection includes fine china from the Orient, tribal artifacts from the Pacific islands, exotic furniture, silver, and even a miniature Taj Mahal carved in ivory. For children, there are several rooms devoted to natural history. The museum is open Monday through Saturday 10:00 a.m. to 5:00 p.m., Sunday noon to 5:00 p.m., and Thursday evenings until 9:00 p.m. Admission is $6 for adults, $3 for senior citizens, students, and for children 6 to 18, and $12 for a family of four.

▲**Salem Maritime National Historic Site**—Run by the
National Park Service at 174 Derby Street, the site includes
the Custom and Derby houses along with several wharves
and warehouses illustrating Salem's former dominance as
a port. It is open daily September through June 8:30 a.m.
to 5:00 p.m. and July 1 through Labor Day 8:30 a.m. to
6:00 p.m. Admission is free.

▲**Salem Wax Museum**—Wax figures represent Salem's
past in a variety of historical scenes that depict the founding of Salem, the witch trials, and the city's prosperous
seafaring days in this museum at 288 Derby Street. A 23-
minute multi-media show on the witch trials is included in
the admission price of $4 for adults, $3.50 for seniors, and
$2.50 for children under 14. Daily hours are 10:00 a.m. to
6:00 p.m. July through October, and 10:00 a.m. to 4:30
p.m. during the rest of the year (weekends only January
through March).

▲▲**The House of Seven Gables**—At 54 Turner Street
on the water, this is the house that inspired Nathaniel
Hawthorne's well-known novel by the same name. The
house was built in 1668 and harbors a secret staircase.
The house in which Hawthorne was born has been
moved to the grounds in recent years, and the complex
includes two other buildings dating back to the 1600s.
You can tour the complex from 9:30 a.m. to 5:30 p.m.
July 1 through Labor Day and from 10:00 a.m. to 4:30 p.m.
during the rest of the year. Admission is $6 for adults,
$2.50 for children 6 to 17. The tour includes a short
introductory film.

Salem also has many notable homes dating from the
1600s through the 1800s which are open to the public.
The **Ropes Mansion**, several doors down from the Witch
House on Essex Street, was built in 1727 and remodeled
in 1894. It is operated by the Essex Institute. It is open
June through October 10:00 a.m. to 4:00 p.m. Tuesday
through Saturday, 1:00 to 4:30 p.m. Sunday. Admission is
$3 for adults, $2.50 for seniors, and $1.50 for children
6 to 16.

You will come across other historic homes as you walk around the town; pick up a visitor map at the Chamber of Commerce in the Town Hall at 32 Derby Square. There is a National Parks Tourist Information Office on Derby Street adjacent to Pickering Wharf, open until 6:00 p.m. in the summer. They can also provide you with information, and there is free parking behind the building. (I have had no trouble parking in the lot for several hours, but you may want to check with the park office to see if there is a time limit on the day of your visit.)

CAPE ANN

Cape Ann is not as well known as Massachusetts' southern cape, Cape Cod, yet it is closer to Boston, and its more rugged coastline typifies, to many, the traditional New England coast. From Cape Ann, you'll travel through a small corner of New Hampshire before entering Maine, or "Vacationland U.S.A." as it bills itself. Many of the heavily touristed areas in Maine are dedicated to the fine art of parting visitors from their cash; that's because many Maine natives make most of their annual income during the three summer months. Steer clear of the factory outlet meccas and enjoy the charm of quaint seacoast towns, the rocky shore, and the sweet smell of pine that permeates the air.

Suggested Schedule

8:30 a.m.	Breakfast.
9:30 a.m	Leave Salem.
10:00 a.m.	Visit Hammond Castle Museum.
11:30 a.m.	Rockport.
1:30 p.m.	Lunch.
3:00 p.m.	Visit Plum Island and Newburyport.
5:00 p.m.	Leave for Kennebunk, Maine.
6:30 p.m.	Check in for the night.

Travel Route: Salem to Kennebunk (100 miles)
Today you'll be traveling along quite a few secondary roads that wind through small towns and at times take sudden turns, making them hard to follow. Watch route signs closely to avoid getting lost. (However, if you have the time, losing oneself on the North Shore can often be a rewarding experience.)

From Salem, take Route 1A north and cross the Beverly Bridge. From there, follow signs to Route 127 north. Driving along Route 127, you'll pass through the lovely towns of Pride's Crossing, Beverly Farms, and Manchester-by-the-Sea, where New England aristocrats hide their stately homes behind stone walls and vast lawns. Pride's

Crossing railroad station has two waiting benches, one earmarked for Democrats and one for Republicans, adding a little humor to the morning commute. Often the most interesting homes and views are just off Route 127, so don't be timid. Try out a few of the more intriguing side streets.

In Manchester, you may want to wake up with an invigorating morning dip at Singing Beach, so called because the moving sand is said to sound like singing when the wind blows. (A warning to non-New Englanders: ocean water north of Boston may be a trifle colder than what you're used to.) Parking at the beach is for residents only, but the ten-minute walk from town is a pleasant one. Just be certain to park legally, for the law has no qualms about ticketing or towing your vehicle.

Continue on Route 127 north to Gloucester, stopping off at Hammond Castle on the way. At Gloucester, take 127A north to Rockport. An art colony for many years, Rockport has become somewhat commercialized recently because of its appealing seaside setting, yet the town still retains much of the charm that originally drew the artists here.

When you're ready to leave Rockport, drive through the center and follow Route 127 back to Gloucester. Four miles out of town there is a turnoff on your right to the village of Annisquam, a sleepy hamlet with beautiful oceanside homes; this route offers a quick scenic detour. Upon reaching Gloucester, take Route 128 south to Exit 14, then Route 133 north to Rowley. (Antique lovers will be pleased to know that Route 133 is lined with antique shops.) At Rowley, follow Route 1A north to Newburyport. From Newburyport, take Route 113 west to Interstate 95 north, following it to Kennebunk, Exit 3 in Maine. Interstate 95 is called the Maine Turnpike once you cross the Maine/New Hampshire state line.

The State of Maine operates an excellent tourist information center in Kittery just a few miles over the state line. Accessible from the highway, it's a good place to pick up a state map ($1) and additional state tourist information from the helpful staff.

The North Shore

Sightseeing Highlights

▲▲The Hammond Castle Museum—The castle, at 80 Hesperus Avenue in Gloucester, was built during the late 1920s, although much of the building and its contents actually date to medieval and Renaissance Europe. The castle was built for John Hays Hammond, Jr. Though not a household name, he holds over 400 patents and is credited with many inventions that have shaped modern life, ranging from radio control systems to shaving cream. The castle interior includes an organ with over 8,000 pipes and, in the center of a medieval courtyard, a reflecting pool that Hammond used to dive into from his second-floor bedroom window. Another unique fixture in the castle is a rain-making system, which Hammond installed in the roof over the courtyard to water his plants. On Route 127, the turnoff to Hesperus Avenue is about 4½

miles from Manchester center on your right. The street
sign is not well marked from this direction, so keep your
eyes peeled. Guided tours are $5 for adults, $4 for students and seniors, $3 for children 6 to 12. The castle
should be open daily from 9:00 a.m. to 5:00 p.m. (last tour
at 4:00 p.m.), but you may want to call ahead (508-283-
7673) to verify hours during your visit, as it sometimes
closes early for special events and opens late if the
employees don't feel like arriving on time. The castle is
closed Thanksgiving, Christmas, and New Year's Day.

▲▲**Plum Island and Parker River National Wildlife
Refuge**—This stop on the itinerary offers car-cramped
legs miles of golden sand beaches to walk on and bird-
watchers an opportunity to see various species in their
natural habitat. The entrance fee is $5 per car, and the
number of cars entering the refuge is sometimes restricted
for environmental reasons. To get there, turn right onto
Rolfe's Lane from Route 1A in Newbury and follow the
signs. One word of caution: in early July the beaches in
this area are visited by "greenheads," a type of horsefly
with a nasty bite. The greenhead season only lasts about
two weeks, and I've been told bug spray will repel
them. Come prepared and you can still appreciate this
beautiful park.

Lodging

When it comes to eating and sleeping in Kennebunk or
Kennebunkport, Kennebunkport gets more tourist traffic,
which means crowds and higher prices. I recommend
staying in quieter Kennebunk, which is also closer to
the highway. **The Kennebunk Inn** on Main Street in
Kennebunk center, built in 1799, is as comfortable and
charming as anything you'll find in neighboring Kennebunkport and less costly. Double rooms range from $89 to
$175 during the summer, and start as low as $49 in the
winter. With the exception of Christmas Day, the inn is
open year-round. There is also an excellent restaurant on
the premises. Call (207) 985-3351 for reservations.

Should you decide to join the "Bush Watchers" in
Kennebunkport (former President George Bush's summer

home is here, and tourism in the town has increased since
he was inaugurated), the Federal-style **Captain Lord
Mansion**, listed on the National Register of Historic
Places, is a good choice. During the summer doubles are
$149 to $199 per night, including a full breakfast (207-
967-3141), and rates are lower in the off-season.

As a last resort, stay at one of the two motels on opposite sides of Exit 3 in Kennebunk. They take advantage of
the overflow from Kennebunkport, so their rates are just
about as high, and even higher than the Kennebunk Inn's
without the ambience.

Camping

Yankeeland Campground is less than 3 miles from
Interstate 95. Get off I-95 north at Exit 3; a right turn at
the end of the exit ramp will take you in the opposite
direction from Kennebunk. Drive straight for 2.7 miles.
The entrance to the campground will be on your left.
Hookups, hot showers, and complete recreational facilities
including swimming are all available. Tent sites are $12
per night, and RV sites are $14 and $16. The campground
is open from May through Columbus Day. For reservations, call (207) 985-7576.

Dining

For lunch, I recommend **Woodman's** on the causeway
in Essex about 3 miles after turning onto Route 133.
Woodman's is a North Shore institution serving phenom-
enal fried clams. Although their prices are no longer dirt
cheap, portions are so large that two people should have
no problem splitting a dinner. If hunger sets in before
you leave Rockport, there are plenty of restaurants on
Bearskin Neck or along Beach Street in the center
of town.

For your evening meal in Kennebunk, **Squaretoes** on
Main Street offers traditional Italian, New England, and
seafood dishes at moderate prices. They also serve decent
breakfasts.

The **Kennebunk Inn** across the street is the place to
go for more refined dining. The menu changes, but New

England specialties are the standard fare. Dinner entrées average $15 to $20.

Itinerary Options

Cape Ann, with its quiet towns and excellent beaches, is a relaxing place to unwind for a few days. Crane's Beach off Route 133 in Ipswich and Good Harbor Beach off Route 127 in Gloucester are two of my favorite beaches in the area. The parking lot at Good Harbor is for residents only, but sometimes you can find parking within walking distance. For a $10 fee, anyone can park at Crane's. On hot summer days, especially weekends, the lot fills up quickly. The Crane Mansion at nearby Castle Hill was built with money made in bathroom fixtures and is now rented out for elegant parties.

Picnics and polo go hand-in-hand at the Myopia Hunt Club. The action usually starts around 3:00 p.m. on Sunday afternoons throughout the summer and early fall. The polo grounds are off Route 1A in Hamilton. Call (508) 468-7956 for information.

Summer whale-watching expeditions are a very popular North Shore pastime. The Yankee Fleet in Gloucester operates both whale-watching cruises and deep-sea fishing trips. Call 800-WHALING or (508) 283-0313 for prices and schedules.

If you do stick around the North Shore for a while, Chipper's River Cafe (508-356-7956) on Market Street in Ipswich has delicious, out-of-the-ordinary sandwiches at reasonable prices. The Wenham Tea House (508-468-1398) serves simple home-cooked meals and corn muffins that will carry you back to your childhood. Wenham also has a small museum with period rooms and a doll collection. The museum is located at 132 Main Street and is open year-round Monday through Friday 11:00 a.m. to 4:00 p.m., Saturday 1:00 to 4:00 p.m., Sunday 2:00 to 5:00 p.m. It is closed on holidays. Admission is $3 for adults, $2.50 for seniors, and $1 for children 6 to 14.

Portsmouth, New Hampshire

Although Portsmouth may not be well known outside New England, it is a gem of a city. In fact, even many

New Englanders aren't aware of this port city's charms, but it is certainly worth a visit if you have time. In addition to an extensive selection of fine shops and restaurants—most notably, the **Blue Strawberry**, which serves fabulous six-course dinners (29 Ceres St. overlooking the water; reservations are a must; 603-431-6420)—Portsmouth boasts an interesting and historic waterfront district.

Strawberry Banke Museum is in the heart of the waterfront district. The museum is really a preserved neighborhood originally settled in the 1630s and so named for the profusion of strawberries that once grew there along the banks of the Piscataqua River. After existing as a thriving community for several centuries, the area gradually deteriorated and faced demolition in the 1950s. A group of concerned citizens stepped in and began creating the museum you see today. Forty-five buildings make up the museum. Some have been decorated with period furnishings, some have costumed guides, some exhibit early American tools or building methods of the day, and a few can only be viewed from the exterior as they are still awaiting restoration. The most interesting buildings at Strawberry Banke include the childhood home of Victorian writer Thomas Bailey Aldrich, the beautiful Goodwin Mansion, the Dinsmore Shop where coopers make the wooden barrels once used extensively for transporting and storing goods, and the Drisco House. The latter, a two-family house built in 1795, is furnished on one side in the style of the 1790s and on the other as it would have appeared in the 1950s, an example of how a house's use would have changed over the years. The museum is open daily 10:00 a.m. to 5:00 p.m. May through October. Admission is $10 for adults, $9 for seniors, $5 for children ages 6 to 17. Admission for families with 2 or more children is $25.

In addition to Strawberry Banke, there are a number of historic homes open to the public throughout the city. The **Moffat-Ladd House and Gardens** (open mid-June through mid-October Monday through Saturday 1:00 to 4:00 p.m., Sunday 2:00 to 5:00 p.m., admission $4 for adults, $1 for children 7 to 12) and the **Wentworth-Gardner House** (open mid-June through September Tuesday through Sunday 1:00 to 4:00 p.m., admission $3 for adults, $1.50 per child) were both built around 1760. A map and guide to the historic properties is available from the Chamber of Commerce (603-436-1118). The **Portsmouth Heritage Museum** has exhibits of local history (603-431-2000).

Portsmouth also has a small **Children's Museum** located at 280 Marcy Street just a few blocks from Strawberry Banke. The museum is open Tuesday through Saturday from 10:00 a.m. to 5:00 p.m., Sunday 1:00 to 5:00 p.m., and Monday during the summer. Admission is $3.50 for both adults and children and $3 for seniors. Children under age 1 are admitted free. At Portsmouth's **Albacore Park**, visitors can tour a 1952 electric and diesel submarine. The park is open from 9:30 a.m. to 4:30 p.m. daily mid-March through November and Wednesday through Sunday December through mid-March. Admission is $4 for adults, $3 for seniors, $2 for children 7 to 12, and $10 for families.

As in many New England cities, harbor and whale-watching cruises leave from the port. **Portsmouth Harbor Cruises** (603-436-8084 or 800-776-0915) operates harbor cruises, and the **Isles of Shoals Steamship Company** runs excursions to the Isles and whale-watch expeditions (603-431-5500 or 800-441-4620). To get to Portsmouth's historic district and waterfront, take Exit 7 off Interstate 95, about 20 miles north of the center of Newburyport. You'll see signs directing you to Strawberry Banke from downtown Portsmouth.

COASTAL MAINE

The object of the day is to travel from Kennebunk to Bar Harbor, about a 4½ hour drive, much of it along Maine's scenic coastline. The best way to enjoy the trip is to follow the travel route at your own pace, seeing what interests you most. Whether it's browsing through Kennebunkport's shops, swimming at Kennebunk Beach in the morning, outlet shopping in Freeport, viewing fine art at the Portland Museum of Art, or picnicking on the harbor in lovely Camden, the day invites you to spend it at your leisure.

Suggested Schedule

9:00 a.m.	Leave Kennebunk.
6:00 p.m.	Arrive in Bar Harbor.

Travel Route: Kennebunk to Bar Harbor (200 miles)
Take the Maine Turnpike (Interstate 95) north from Kennebunk. If you wish to make a stop in Portland, take Interstate 295 at Exit 6A; otherwise continue on I-95 north. Although Portland is Maine's largest city, it is still small enough that any exit for downtown will take you to the center of Portland as long as you drive east. The **Old Port Exchange District** on the waterfront is being revitalized, the **Children's Museum of Maine** (open daily from 9:30 a.m. to 4:30 p.m., $2.50 per person over 1 year old) at 746 Stevens Avenue might be a mandatory stop if you're traveling with small children, and the **Portland Museum of Art** (open Tuesday through Saturday 10:00 a.m. to 5:00 p.m., Sunday from noon to 5:00 p.m., $3.50 for adults, $2.50 for seniors and students, $1 for children under 18, and free on Thursday evenings from 5:00 to 9:00 p.m.) at Congress and High streets has a wonderful collection of Winslow Homer paintings and is well respected in art circles. Interstate 295 will take you back to the turnpike if you just continue north.

Fans of L.L. Bean and designer outlets might want to stop in the once-sleepy town of Freeport, now a mile-long

The Maine Coast

strip of names like Ralph Lauren, Anne Klein, and
Benetton. Good bargains can be found, and a midnight
shopping spree at L.L. Bean (open 24 hours) is a rite of
passage for any New England college student. To stop in
Freeport, take Exit 19 off the turnpike. You can shop your
way through Freeport and get right back on the highway
at Exit 20 on the other end of town. If shopping is not
your bag, the **Freeport Balloon Company** (207-865-
1712) operates hot-air balloon rides that will take you far
from the shopping mecca below.

Everyone should leave the turnpike at Exit 22 for Bath,
Brunswick, and coastal Route 1. Follow Route 1 all the
way up to Ellsworth, passing through the towns of
Wiscasset, "the prettiest town in Maine" with a number of
historic homes including the striking **Castle Tucker** overlooking Wiscasset Harbor (open Tuesday through
Saturday 11:00 a.m. to 4:00 p.m. during July and August,
admission is $2 for adults and 50 cents for children to 12),
Rockport (nestled in a quiet cove about a mile off Route
1), and Camden (with its harbor park overlooking
Penobscot Bay). The drive from Freeport to Camden takes
a little under two hours without stops, and it is about

1½ hours more from Camden to Bar Harbor. From Rockport on, you'll catch tantalizing glimpses of the sea all along the route. Flea market buffs will find Route 1 in Searsport absolute heaven.

Those with extra time may fancy a detour onto Route 27 east and the Boothbay Peninsula, where scenic coves, quaint shops, and art galleries await visitors. There are two aquariums in the area—the **Marine Aquarium** run by the Maine Department of Marine Resources in West Boothbay Harbor (open daily Memorial Day through Labor Day with free admission) and **Oceans East Aquarium** at 87 Atlantic Avenue in Boothbay Harbor (207-633-3965). At **Railway Village** on Route 27, you can ride a narrow gauge steam train and see a fine collection of vintage autos (open daily 9:00 a.m. to 5:00 p.m. from mid-June through mid-October; admission $5 for adults, $2 for children).

At Ellsworth, take Route 3 east for the final 20-mile leg of the journey to Bar Harbor.

Lodging
Many of the lodgings in Bar Harbor are open during the summer months only, so be sure to call ahead if you are traveling during the off-season.

For my money, **Daney's Cottage** (207-288-3856), on quiet, residential Hancock Street, is about the best bargain around at $15 per person. You may have to give up the luxury of a private bath, but rooms are clean and downtown Bar Harbor is only a five-minute walk. The **Mount Desert Island Hostel** on Kennebec Street has dormitory beds for about $10 per night. The hostel is open only during the summer, and reservations are recommended (207-288-5587). The **Bar Harbor Inn**, in the heart of downtown right on the harbor, offers fancier accommodations. Doubles range from $95 to $209 (207-288-3351 or 800-248-3351).

Mt. Desert Street, also convenient to downtown, has a whole string of inns. Some of the rooms at the Victorian **Mira Monte Inn** (207-288-4263) have fireplaces, and a breakfast buffet is included in the room rate ($115-$140)

Holbrook House (207-288-4970 or 800-695-1120) has wonderful porches, and all rooms have private baths. Rates including a full breakfast range from $110 to $225. The attractive **Primrose Cottage Inn** (207-288-4031 or 800-543-7842) is a pleasant establishment, where rooms are priced from $85 to $140.

There are countless motels and cottages along Route 3 as you approach Bar Harbor from Ellsworth. If you're not planning to visit during the month of August or on a holiday weekend, you can probably check into any of these without advance reservations. The Bar Harbor Chamber of Commerce will send you free of charge a useful brochure with detailed lodging listings. Write to them at P.O. Box 158, Bar Harbor, ME 04609, or call (207) 288-5103, for your copy. If you plan to visit during the winter months, be sure to call ahead as many businesses close at the end of October.

Northeast Harbor, only 12 miles farther on Route 3 from Bar Harbor, can be a welcome alternative to Bar Harbor's summer throngs and is equally convenient to Acadia. If your budget permits, the view of the harbor from **The Asticou** (207-276-3344) is first-rate and so is the service. It is best to book well in advance, particularly for August, and the oceanside rooms naturally fill up first. Double rooms start around $200 mid-June through mid-September and cost substantially less during the off-season. In the center of Northeast Harbor, **The Maison Suisse Inn** (207-276-5223) provides attractive guest rooms complete with four-poster beds and cozy down comforters to take the nip out of the Maine night air. The inn is open seasonally from May through October. Double rooms start at $105 and suites at $165, breakfast included, in peak summer season.

Camping
Blackwoods Campground, about 8 miles from Bar Harbor and one mile from Seal Harbor off Route 3, is the only campground in the heart of Acadia National Park. Several miles from the Seal Harbor entrance to Acadia, it is operated by the National Park Service. The sites are

more heavily wooded than in most private campgrounds in the area, and there's a path to the ocean. Reservations must be made through Ticketron outlets or by mail up to eight weeks ahead, and it is recommended that they be made at least three weeks ahead. It may be possible to obtain a site on a space-available basis upon your arrival. Generally, the earlier in the day you arrive, the better chance you'll have of success. There are bathrooms on the premises and a shower nearby. For provisions, there is a small store in Seal Harbor, and you'll find more substantial offerings at the Pine Tree Market on Main Street in Northeast Harbor about 4 miles away. Write Acadia National Park, P.O. Box 177, Bar Harbor, ME 04609, for reservations and current rate information.

There are a number of campgrounds reasonably close to Bar Harbor on Route 3 between Bar Harbor and Ellsworth. **Bar Harbor Campground** (207-288-5185) is only 4 miles from the center of town and 3 miles from the main entrance to Acadia. Sites are around $18 per night. It has modern facilities including a heated pool. **Mount Desert Narrows Camping Resort** (207-288-4782), 8 miles from Bar Harbor, has RV hookups and ocean sites available ($18-$35 per night). **Barcadia Campground** (207-288-3520) is about 10 miles from Bar Harbor on the water. Sites are about $18 per night.

Dining
No trip to the Maine seacoast is complete without a lobster dinner, and **Abel's Lobster Pound** on Route 198 in Mount Desert won't disappoint you. Abel's is open for dinner only. Reservations are recommended; call (207) 276-5827.

The **Reading Room** at the **Bar Harbor Inn** (207-288-3351) at the base of Main Street and the **Rinehart Dining Pavilion** (207-288-5663) on Eden Street in Bar Harbor both offer quality dining with arresting ocean views. While seafood dominates their menus, landlubbers will enjoy the Rinehart's Prime Rib. **George's** (207-288-4505), at 7 Stephen's Lane behind the First National Bank on Main Street, is not situated on the water, but its elegant ambience and unique presentation of traditional dishes warrant a visit. Dinner entrées start at about $15 in all three restaurants.

For more moderately priced meals, **Testa's** (207-288-3327) on Main Street has been a Bar Harbor institution for over 50 years specializing in family-style Italian cuisine and seafood dishes. Dinner entrées start around $8. **Jordan's Restaurant**, farther down Cottage Street at number 80, is *the* spot to go for breakfast. Jordan's is known for the best "blues" on the island, meaning blueberry muffins. Their blueberry pancakes are also tasty. They do a brisk business, so service is fast and curt (207-288-3586).

Itinerary Options

There are several islands off the Maine coast that make for enjoyable summer day excursions if your schedule allows. Because of its unspoiled beauty, Monhegan has long been an artists' retreat; you can visit this small rocky island by boat. The *Balmy Days II* leaves Boothbay Harbor from Pier 8 daily at 9:30 a.m. during the summer. Call (207) 633-2284 for reservations and ticket information. Bring a good pair of walking shoes as cars are not allowed on the island.

Ferries travel to Vinalhaven and North Haven from Rockland several times a day year-round; trips take about an hour and fifteen minutes. Call (207) 596-2202 for departure and ticket information. The exclusive Islesboro is only a 20-minute ferry ride from Lincolnville Beach north of Camden and may be the best island destination if your time is limited. The Blue Heron (207-734-6611) restaurant is the island's most popular dining establishment if you decide against a beach picnic. Call (207) 789-5611 for ferry ticket information.

Many find the Maine coast most captivating from the sea, making windjammer cruises a favored pastime. Maine Windjammer Cruises in Camden operate 3- and 6-day cruises with rates ranging from $325 to $625 per person (207-236-2938 or 800-736-7981). Bring lots of warm clothing if you opt for one of these scenic cruises. It can get very chilly on the water, even in midsummer.

ACADIA NATIONAL PARK

Acadia National Park is the easternmost national park in the country. If you stand atop Cadillac Mountain at dawn, they say you can be the first person in the United States to see the sunrise. The park, which encompasses rocky coastline, sheltered coves, wooded mountain trails, fresh-water lakes, and ocean vistas, was donated by conservation-minded individuals to create a national park, rather than being purchased outright by the government. Today you'll see why they felt the land should be preserved.

Suggested Schedule

9:00 a.m.	Start your day in Acadia at the visitor information center, then enter the Park Loop Road.
1:00 p.m.	Picnic lunch on scenic Somme Sound.
3:30 p.m.	Enjoy tea on the lawn at the Jordan Pond Restaurant.
5:00 p.m.	Drive to Cadillac Mountain summit.
7:00 p.m.	Have a light dinner and stroll by Bar Harbor's many souvenir shops.

Travel Route

You'll drive about 50 miles before the day is over, all within the relatively small area of Mount Desert Island. Start the drive at Acadia's visitor information center, 3 miles west of Bar Harbor just off Route 3. After leaving the visitor's center, take the Park Loop Road in the direction of Sand Beach.

Visit the Wild Garden, Abbe Museum, Sand Beach, and Thunder Hole, then exit the park road at Seal Harbor and drive 3 miles to Northeast Harbor on Route 3. From the center of Northeast Harbor, follow signs to Sargent Drive which will take you by some of the more exclusive residences. Just past the Tennis Club, a turnout on your left offers a view overlooking Somme Sound, the only natural

Acadia National Park

MOUNT
DESERT
ISLAND

FRENCHMAN
BAY

Visitor Center
Start of Park
Loop Road

Ferry to
Nova Scotia

Bar Harbor

Cadillac Mt.
Entrance

To
Southwest
Harbor

Park
Headquarters

Acadia
Wild Garden
Abbe Museum

Park Loop
Road

Cadillac
Mt.

The
Bubbles

Park Loop
Road

ACADIA NATIONAL PARK

Sand Beach

Jordan Pond
House

Thunder Hole

Sargent Drive

SOMES SOUND

Seal
Harbor

Blackwoods

Otter Point

Stanley
Brook
Entrance

Northeast
Harbor

Seal
Harbor

ATLANTIC
OCEAN

fiord on the east coast. The spot is ideal for a picnic; just
be sure to save room for afternoon tea.

If you're traveling by camper, motorcycle, or recreational vehicle, you'll need to retrace your steps at this
point to the Stanley Brook entrance to Acadia (where you
exited for Seal and Northeast harbors) as only automobiles
are allowed on Sargent Drive and traveling it on foot is
impractical. By car, follow Sargent Drive along majestic
Somme Sound until it intersects with Route 3. Take Route
3 back to Northeast Harbor, reenter Park Loop Road at the
Stanley Brook entrance, drive to Jordan Pond, perhaps

stopping for tea, then continue on the park road to the
turnoff for Cadillac Mountain. After visiting the summit,
return to the Park Loop Road, then exit onto Route 233
to return to Bar Harbor.

Sightseeing Highlights
▲▲▲**Acadia National Park**—This park covers more than
35,000 acres. The largest portion of the park, and the most
heavily touristed, is on Mount Desert Island, so named for
its treeless top by French explorer Samuel de Champlain
in the early 1600s. Frenchman's Bay, whose name also
derives from the French Colonial era, lies between Mount
Desert Island and the Schoodic Peninsula, where there is
an extension of Acadia. Entrance to the park is $5 per car
for a seven-day pass. Be sure to bring your binoculars
as seals and otters can often be seen playing on rocks
just offshore.

The visitor information center is a good place to famil-
iarize yourself with the park. A 15-minute introductory
film to Acadia is shown every half hour. Pick up a free
map while you are here, and a list of hiking trails if you
wish to stray from the main road.

The **Wild Garden** is one of the first detours along the
park loop. Plants you'll see throughout in this garden of
wildflowers are labeled, making them easier to identify
when you spot them in their natural habitat. The **Abbe
Museum**, at the same turnoff, is a small museum of tools
and artifacts used by the Indians who were the island's
first settlers. The museum is open during the summer
months and has a small admission charge.

Back on the loop, you come to **Sand Beach**, unusual
because most beaches you see on Mount Desert Island are
rugged and rocky. Even on the hottest of summer days,
this beach is kept cool by ocean breezes. The trail to
Great Head starts at the far end of the beach. Farther
along the park road is **Thunder Hole**, where wave erosion has created a hole in the rocks which resounds with
a booming noise as the waves crash to the shore.

The restaurant at **Jordan Pond** serves a marvelous
afternoon tea on the lawn with a splendid view of the

pond and the "Bubbles"—two matching rounded mountains shaped by glaciers. If solitude is more your cup of tea, take a leisurely walk on the nature trail or on one of the flat paths alongside the pond. Find your own secluded rock and just soak up the scenery. The **Gate House** across the road from the restaurant is also worth a closer look because of its unique stone architecture.

The drive to **Cadillac Summit** will be the high point of your day both figuratively and literally, as it is the highest point on the Atlantic coast. Though an uninterrupted climb by automobile takes only about ten minutes, scores of breathtaking vistas will no doubt slow your progress. (The climb and descent will put a strain on your vehicle so be sure to check the fluids and brakes before starting the ascent.) An arresting panorama awaits atop Cadillac Mountain. (Both the mountain and the luxury automobile were named after the same Frenchman.) From the summit one can see the harbors below, the Porcupine and Cranberry islands dotting the foreground, and Winter Harbor, Ironbound, and Schoodic across Frenchman's Bay. The view is particularly spectacular at sunrise or sunset, and the summit is also a popular star-gazing post. The road is closed from midnight until one hour before sunrise.

Helpful Hints

Many people choose to see Acadia from a bicycle rather than through a windshield. Except for the road to Cadillac Summit, which is demanding enough for a four-cylinder engine, two-wheel transportation is a refreshing way to explore the park. Bicycles and mountain bikes can be rented in Bar Harbor from **Acadia Bike & Canoe** at 48 Cottage Street (207-288-9605 or 800-526-8615). **Bar Harbor Bicycle Shop** at 141 Cottage Street rents bikes for about $14 per day and multi-day rates are available (207-288-0342).

A sightseeing cruise on Frenchman's Bay is another agreeable way to survey the park and islands. **Frenchman's Bay Boating Company** next to the municipal pier in Bar Harbor offers a variety of cruising options. Call (207) 288-3322 for more information. The ***Natalie Todd*** is a three-masted schooner that also has cruises on the bay. A two-hour sail is $16 for adults and $10 for children (207-288-4585).

Just for Kids

About 12 miles west of Bar Harbor on Route 3, a 3-mile stretch of highway has enough mini-golf courses, ice cream parlors, paddle boats, go-cart tracks, water slide parks, and even a small zoo to bring just about any travel-weary child out of the doldrums.

Itinerary Options

Those with more time may wish to go on to Southwest and Bass harbors and the western part of Acadia from Northeast Harbor, rather than return to the main Park Loop Road immediately. From Bass Harbor you can take a ferry to Swan's Island, and another ferry operates from Northeast Harbor to the Cranberry Islands. There are also over 120 miles of trails within Acadia to tempt the hiker. If you are so inclined and have the opportunity to stay a day or two longer, investigate some of them on your own.

Schoodic Peninsula, directly across Frenchman's Bay from Bar Harbor, is also part of Acadia National Park. Because of its distance from the heart of Acadia, Schoodic is much less traveled but no less scenic. Take an extra day to traverse this more remote part of the park and the quiet fishing village of Winter Harbor. To get there, you'll need to take Route 3 back to Ellsworth and continue on US 1 north to West Gouldsboro. From there take Route 186 to Winter Harbor.

For those with lots of time on their hands, Nova Scotia is just a 6-hour ferry ride from Bar Harbor on the *Bluenose.* From mid-June through mid-September, the famous ferry departs daily for Yarmouth at 8:00 a.m. One-way passenger fare is $40 for adults, $20 for children 5 to 12. Automobiles and mobile homes up to 20 feet cost $74 one-way. Round-trip fares are $70 for adults, $35 for children, and $129.50 for cars. The ferry runs on a reduced schedule the rest of the year, and fares are lower. Call (800) 341-7981 or (207) 288-3397 for further information

and reservations. Gambling is allowed on board once the
ship reaches international waters. In Nova Scotia, the most
scenic routes are along the coasts. The Cabot Trail on
Cape Breton at the easternmost end of Nova Scotia is generally considered to be the province's most beautiful
region. From Caribou, Nova Scotia, you can take the ferry
to sleepy Prince Edward Island where deserted white sand
beaches meet a surprisingly warm, blue sea.

MT. WASHINGTON

The trip across Maine, approximately 4 hours from Bar Harbor to Bethel, is the longest stretch of straight driving without a stop on the entire trip. However, as you approach the White Mountains, the views make the journey quite a pleasant one. The beauty of western Maine and New Hampshire's White Mountain National Forest is today's focal point.

Suggested Schedule

7:30 a.m.	Early breakfast at Jordan's.
8:30 a.m.	Leave Bar Harbor.
12:30 p.m.	Lunch in Bethel, Maine.
2:30 p.m.	Take the auto road to the top of Mt. Washington, the highest peak in the northeastern United States.
6:00 p.m.	Check into your accommodations.
7:00 p.m.	Dine in either Jackson or North Conway.

Travel Route: Bar Harbor to Mt. Washington (200 miles)

Take Route 3 west from Bar Harbor to Ellsworth. At Ellsworth, follow US 1A toward Bangor. Just before Bangor, take Interstate 395 west, to US 2, which will take you all the way to Gorham, New Hampshire. In the center of Gorham, turn left onto Route 16 south. The entrance to the Mt. Washington Auto Road is about 8 miles from Gorham on your right. After a stop at Mt. Washington, take Route 16 to Jackson or continue to North Conway.

Sightseeing information is not the only reason to stop at the information center on Route 16 in Intervale just outside North Conway. The panorama of the Mt. Washington Valley from the parking lot is one of the finest around.

Sightseeing Highlights

▲▲▲**Mt. Washington**—At 6,288 feet, this is the highest peak in the Northeast, and on clear days, the panoramas from the ascent and summit are unrivaled. On top are a weather station and complete tourist facilities. Even in July the peak's climate can be quite brisk, so be sure to bring warm clothing with you. The summit can be reached by the auto road in your own vehicle at a cost of $12 for car and driver, plus $5 for each additional adult, $3 for children 5 to 12. The auto road is open from mid-May to mid-October, weather permitting. However, you should not take those bumper stickers that read "This Car Climbed Mt. Washington" lightly; the climb to the top is not easy, even for an automobile in top-notch condition. Should you prefer not to put the wear and tear on your car, vans are available to take riders up the mountain: $17 for adults, $10 for children 5 to 12. After five hours on the road, you may find it a welcome relief to let a tour guide do the driving. There is also cog-railway service available from the other side of Mt. Washington at Bretton Woods. The round-trip by rail costs $32 for adults and takes three hours.

Of course, many hikers try their luck at climbing the mountain. Should you wish to do so, you'll need a whole day. The information center across from the entrance to the auto road can suggest trails that are right for your ability. It is fairly easy for weary hikers to get rides back down the mountain from people who have taken the auto road. Camping shelters along the trail provide sanctuary for hikers who get caught in bad weather or who just want to spend more time exploring the region.

▲**Gondola Skyride**—For a different perspective of Mt. Washington, take the gondola at Wildcat Ski Area, which faces the mountain. The ride operates on weekends Memorial Day through late June, and daily during July, August, and September from 10:00 a.m. to 4:30 p.m. and on weekends only during June. Tickets are $8 for adults, $3.50 for children 7 to 11.

Jackson

About 8 miles south of Wildcat is a covered bridge leading to the town of Jackson. Although Jackson does have Black Mountain downhill ski area, the town is best known as a

cross-country skiers' haven, so there are plenty of cozy
bed and breakfasts around to take care of tired winter and
summer visitors alike.

North Conway

Mt. Cranmore in nearby North Conway is one of the oldest ski areas in the Northeast. Although rail service is no
longer available, trains used to arrive from Boston on a
regular basis, dropping skiers off right in the heart of the
village. For this reason, the town has been catering to
tourists for many years and the effects are beginning to
show. In the past ten years, factory outlets and the multi-
tude of shoppers they bring have begun to crowd the
town's charming core. Still, North Conway has its appeal,
which includes the greatest variety of shops, restaurants,
and lodging establishments in the Mt. Washington valley.

▲**Cathedral Ledge**—Just a few minutes from the center
of North Conway, the ledge draws throngs of rock
climbers and spectators alike. You'll probably find this
daring sport fascinating to watch if you've never witnessed
it first-hand. Climbers can be observed from below, or you
can drive up the road to the top of the ledge and congrat-
ulate the climbers as they reach their goal. Cool off after
watching the climbers with a swim at neighboring Echo
Lake State Park.

▲**The Conway Scenic Railroad**—The railroad runs out
of North Conway's picturesque depot, which was built in
1874, travels south along the Saco River, crosses the Swift
River to the town of Conway, and is enjoyable to young
and old alike. Tickets for the one-hour excursion are $7.50
for adults, $5 for children 4 to 12. First-class tickets in the
"Gertrude Emma," a 92-year-old restored parlor car, cost
an additional $3. Departure times are 10:00 a.m. and 12:00,
2:00, and 4:00 p.m. daily from mid-May through October,
on Thanksgiving weekend, and on weekends November
and December through Christmas. In July and August there
is also the Sunset Special, which leaves on Tuesday,
Wednesday, Thursday, and Saturday nights at 6:30 p.m.
Call (603) 356-5251 or (800) 232-5251 for information.

Mt. Washington Valley

There is plenty for children to do in the valley. **Storyland** (on Route 16 in Glen), is an amusement park where storybook characters come to life, and is a favorite of youngsters. It is open daily from Father's Day to Labor Day and on weekends only Labor Day through Columbus Day (603-383-4293). Four miles west of the junction of US 302 and Route 16, **Attitash Ski Area** in Bartlett operates an alpine slide and water park during the summer. There is a mountain stream swimming hole at Jackson. Just follow the signs from Jackson center toward the Eagle Mountain House. The swimming hole is about halfway up the hill on your right.

Lodging

The **Eagle Mountain House** in Jackson is a charming resort on a quiet country road with beautiful mountain views. The rooms in the recently restored hotel are comfortably elegant and a relative bargain, starting at $105 during the height of fall foliage season and $65 during early spring and late fall. Suites start at $155 during the summer and $110 in off-season. Tennis, golf, and swimming are all available at the resort as well. Follow signs up Carter Notch Road from the center of Jackson. Call (800) 777-1700 or (603) 383-9111 for reservations.

The **Inn at Thorn Hill**, in a home designed by renowned architect Stanford White, is another lovely lodging option in Jackson village. Rooms are tastefully decorated with Victorian furnishings, and rates starting at $65 per person include lodging, a hearty breakfast, and gourmet evening meal (603-383-4242 or 800-289-8990).

The **Cranmore Inn**, only one block from the center of North Conway on Kearsarge Street, is more reasonably priced than many other inns in town yet offers the same services. A comfortable room for two costs from $35 to $85 per night (depending on the season) including an ample breakfast in the inn's sunny breakfast room. There are several sitting rooms and a swimming pool on the premises. Mt. Cranmore ski area is only five minutes away. Call (603) 356-5502 or (800) 526-5502 for reservations.

Route 16 in North Conway is lined with inns and motels, which can fill up at the height of fall foliage or for big ski weekends. If you're calling ahead, try the **Scottish Lion** (603-356-6381). The rooms are pleasant, meals have a Scottish slant, and there is a lively pub to unwind in after a long day of sightseeing or skiing. Rooms including a full breakfast range from $50 to $100. The inn also operates a Scottish import shop next door. The **White Trellis Motel**, which has pleasant mountain views, makes more of an effort than most to create an attractive atmosphere with flowering window boxes and ivy covered trellises. Doubles range from $38 to $85 depending on the season (603-356-2492). You might also want to try booking a room through Country Inns in the White Mountains, an association of fourteen area inns (603-356-9460 or 800-562-1300).

Camping

Dolly Copp Campground is a national forest campground with 176 sites near the base of Mt. Washington off Route 16, 6 miles south of Gorham. Reservations can be made by the MISTIX reservation system (800-283-CAMP). If you arrive without a reservation, sites are assigned on a first-come, first-served basis. RVs are allowed, but hot showers and electrical hookups are not available. Sites cost about $10 per night. The campground is open from mid-May to mid-October.

Glen Ellis Family Campground, on US 302 just west of the Route 16 junction, is convenient to Jackson, North Conway, and tomorrow's travel route. In case you are low on provisions, there is a supermarket located next to the entrance. The campground itself has complete sanitary and recreational facilities. Sites start at $14 per night, and some are adjacent to the Saco River. The campground operates seasonally from Memorial Day to Columbus Day, July being the busiest month. Call (603) 383-9320 for information in season or (516) 746-2759 for inquiries during the winter.

Dining

The **Millbrook Tavern** at the Bethel Inn in Bethel, Maine, is a good place to stop for lunch. The inn is open year-round, and outdoor dining on the terrace is available during the summer months. Lunch prices start at $5 for sandwiches. Those with extra time, and golf clubs or tennis rackets, might choose to make use of the inn's sports facilities. The inn is also an agreeable home base should you wish to linger in the area. If you are traveling with your own provisions, there are plenty of picnic areas along US 2 that can accommodate an *alfresco* meal nicely.

For dinner, there is fine dining in Jackson at the **Eagle Mountain House**. More moderately priced meals can be had at the **Thompson House Eatery** right in the center of Jackson (603-383-9341). Not too far from Jackson, the **Bernerhof Inn** on US 302 west in Glen, just 2 miles from the Route 16 intersection, serves appetizing European dishes with a German flair, and also has accommodations for overnight guests (603-383-4414 or 800-548-8007).

In North Conway just across from the railroad depot on Main Street, **Horsefeathers**' menu ranges from deluxe burgers to pasta and chicken entrées. The tavern atmosphere is lively, and prices are moderate at $4.95 to $12.95 (603-356-6862). Also in North Conway's center on Seavey Street one block up from Main Street, **Bellini's** serves Italian specialties including homemade pastas prepared in delicious combinations. Try the fettucini with prosciutto, spinach, and mushrooms in a light cream sauce. If you have room, their desserts are also scrumptious. Dinner entrées range from $7.95 to $16.95 (603-356-7000). For reasonably priced blueberry pancake and omelet breakfasts, try the **Big Pickle Restaurant** next door to Bellini's on Seavey Street.

The Arts

The Eastern Slope Playhouse next door to the Eastern Slope Inn on Main Street in North Conway presents professional musical productions during the summer months. Call (603) 356-5776 for schedule and ticket information.

Itinerary Options

The Oxford Hills region of Maine near Bethel, with beautiful freshwater Lakes Norway, Thompson, and Long, a
mineral- and gem-rich landscape, and numerous wooded
trails, is a pleasant place for hikers, rock-hounds, and
fishermen to spend some extra time.

More adventurous travelers may find a river trip to their
liking. **Saco Bound** in Conway, New Hampshire, operates
a variety of river trips including whitewater and flat-water,
by raft or canoe, for several hours or several days. Contact
them at (603) 447-2177 or Box 119, Center Conway, NH
03813, for more details.

WHITE MOUNTAIN NATIONAL FOREST

The White Mountain National Forest is a 750,000-acre expanse in central New Hampshire which encompasses much of the Presidential Range, including 6,288-foot Mt. Washington, as well as a bounty of alpine lakes, streams, cascades, and hiking trails. Today you'll explore this lush region before crossing the border into Vermont.

Suggested Schedule

8:00 a.m.	Breakfast.
9:00 a.m.	Spend the morning and early afternoon savoring the White Mountain National Forest's natural attractions. Enjoy a picnic lunch with an alpine backdrop.
2:00 p.m.	Leave the national forest and travel to Woodstock, Vermont, pausing along the way to visit a mine, a maple sugarhouse, a glassblowing exhibit, or an early farm museum, or hike to the bottom of a gorge.
6:00 p.m.	Check into your lodging.
7:00 p.m.	Dinner.

Travel Route: Jackson/North Conway to Woodstock, Vermont (150 miles)

Route 16 south from Jackson or north from North Conway intersects with US 302 at Glen. Take US 302 west toward Bartlett and Twin Mountain. You will be passing through Crawford Notch State Park. At Twin Mountain, take US 3 south until it merges with Franconia Notch Parkway. Continue south on the parkway, exiting to see the forest's natural attractions. Exits are marked, and parking is provided.

Leaving Franconia Notch State Park, stay on US 3 south to Interstate 93 south. The mountain views from I-93 are breathtaking. Exit I-93 at Route 104 west. At Danbury, proceed on US 4 west all the way to Woodstock, Vermont.

The White Mountains

Alternate Route: From Lincoln just below the Flume, take Route 112 west to Route 118 south. At Warren, Route 118 merges with Route 25. Continue south to Wentworth, then follow Route 25A west to Fairlee, and from there take Route 10 south to Hanover, home of **Dartmouth College**, the Ivy League's northernmost member. The **Hood Museum of Art** at Dartmouth has European, African, and American pieces, as well as works by twentieth-century artists including Picasso, and the **Baker Memorial Library** has Orozco frescoes.

After visiting Hanover, cross the Connecticut River to Norwich, Vermont. From Norwich, follow US 5 south to White River Junction where you can pick up US 4 west to Woodstock. This alternate route enables you to see the lovely college town of Hanover but will not save you any time over the main travel route.

Crawford Notch State Park is in the heart of the White Mountain National Forest. As you travel through the park, you'll pass two small waterfalls, the Silver and Flume cascades, that slither rather than plunge down the mountainside. Both have parking areas. The better mountain view is from the Flume Cascade parking lot. The park's information center is located in a colorful train station near Twin Mountain.

As you near Twin Mountain, there is a striking view of the Mt. Washington Hotel at Bretton Woods. Built in 1902, the hotel was designed to entice the privileged set, and it still holds a commanding presence over the valley. In its heyday, visitors came by the trainload to visit the hotel. Today Bretton Woods is a thriving cross-country ski mecca. The entrance to the **Cog Railway** that climbs Mt. Washington is just beyond the hotel. Trains run every hour on the hour, and the three-hour round-trip to the summit costs $32 for adults, $30 for seniors, $22 for children 7 to 15, children under 6 free. The train runs from early May to mid-November. The railway recommends advance ticket purchase. Call (800) 922-8825 or (603) 846-5404, ext. 7, for reservations.

Cannon Mountain Ski Area is at the northern entrance to **Franconia Notch State Park**. Cannon operates a tramway during nonskiing months ($7 for adults, $3.50 for children 6 to 12; combination tickets to the tram and the Flume are $10 for adults, $5 for children). While at Cannon, you can also visit the **New England Ski Museum** to learn more about the regional history of the sport through an audiovisual presentation. The museum is open from mid-May through mid-October, and again just after Christmas for the winter ski season, from noon to 5 00 p.m., closed on Wednesday. Admission is by donation.

The turnoff to **Old Man of the Mountain** is just after Cannon Mountain and **Echo Lake**. This portion of cliffs overlooking **Profile Lake** was so named because erosion has given the granite the appearance of an old man from certain angles. Nathaniel Hawthorne wrote about the famous formation in his short story, "The Great Stone Face." You will see the old man's profile on many of New Hampshire's highway route signs.

Other highlights of the park include **the Basin** and **the Flume**. Swirling with water, the Basin is a natural pothole formed by ice age glaciers and mountain cascades. There is wheelchair access. Swimming is prohibited. A well-maintained bike path runs through this section of the park, and hiking trails abound. You may wish to hike one of the trails that leave from the Basin area, which are free and likely to be less crowded than the Flume trail.

The Flume is a narrow, moss-covered granite gorge discovered in 1808 by Jesse Guernsey, a 93-year-old woman who was hoping to find a prime fishing spot. After hiking the Flume, you can return to the visitors center or continue on the trail to view a waterfall and natural pool. Plan to spend about an hour and a half here if you decide to hike the entire loop. Although there are buses that can take you from the visitors center halfway to the Flume, much of the arduous walking still lies ahead, and there is no handicapped access. The trail is refreshingly cool on hot summer days, but on brisk autumn days you may want to bring an extra sweater or jacket along. The Flume is open from 9:00 a.m. to 4:30 p.m. daily, June through October. There is a separate admission charge of $5 for adults, $2.50 for children 6 to 12, if you decided not to purchase combination tickets at the Cannon Mountain tram.

In contrast to the park's natural attractions, there is a small amusement park, Fantasy Farm, a waterslide park, and the Whale's Tail, on US 3 just below the Flume.

Rock collectors may want to stop at **Ruggles Mine** near Grafton off US 4 between Interstate 93 and White River Junction. The mine first opened in 1803 and is known for its vast supply of mica. Visitors are allowed to take home mineral samples that they collect, probably accounting for the mine's steep admission charge ($9 for adults, $4 for children 4 to 11). The mine is open on weekends only from mid-May through mid-June, daily mid-June through mid-October 9:00 a.m. to 5:00 p.m.

Just after you pass into Quechee, Vermont, on US 4, only a few miles from the Vermont/New Hampshire state line, there is an information booth on your left. Several hundred yards beyond that, a bridge crosses the dramatic **Quechee Gorge**, 165 feet deep. Parking is available on both sides of the bridge. Take the 1-mile hike to the bottom of the gorge, or just stretch your legs on the short (one-quarter mile) hike to view the waterfall that empties into the river below. There are picnic tables adjacent to the gorge.

A right-hand turn at the first blinking light after the gorge bridge will take you through one of New England's rustic covered bridges and into "downtown" Quechee. There, **Simon Pearce** has completely renovated the old mill so today you can watch glassblowers and potters at their crafts. You can also inspect the modern hydraulic power system that now fuels the ovens. The handmade glassware and pottery is sold in the gift shop along with natural fiber fabrics. The shop is open from 10:00 a.m. to 5:00 p.m., and you can watch glassblowing during those same hours, except from 1:00 to 2:00 p.m. when the craftsmen take their lunch. Admission is free. There is a fine restaurant on the premises as well.

From Simon Pearce, continue on River Road for several miles past lush green golf courses and farms. Should you wish to visit a maple sugarhouse to learn about processing the sweet syrup, turn onto Hillside Road and follow signs to **Sugarbush Farm**. Although sugaring season is in the spring, the farm is open year-round and also makes tasty Vermont cheeses. Call (802) 457-1757 for hours of operation during your visit. Should you visit Sugarbush Farm, return to River Road and cross the Taftsville Covered Bridge, which will take you back onto US 4. Woodstock is only 3 miles west.

Woodstock appears to be the type of town that crime or hardship never touches, a model New England town with elegant Federal-style homes surrounding the Town Green where every blade of grass seems perfectly groomed. Some of the bells in Woodstock's churches were made by Paul Revere himself. A tourist information booth right on the Green will provide answers to questions. The booth is open from 10:00 a.m. to 6:00 p.m. The Town Crier Chalk Board in the center of the business district lists the goings-on for the day.

The **Billings Farm & Museum** is off Route 12 north of Woodstock. The farm offers a look at rural Vermont life of a century ago. You can help hand-churn butter, see how cows were milked the old-fashioned way, and watch woodcarving demonstrations. The farm is open daily from early May through late October from 10:00 a.m. to 5:00 p.m. Admission is $6 for adults, $4.80 for seniors, $3 for children 6 to 17, or $15 for a family.

The Woodstock Historical Society operates the **Dana House Museum** at 26 Elm Street. Woodstock artifacts, period furnishings, antique costumes, tools, and toys make up the majority of the exhibits. The museum is open May through October, Monday through Saturday 10:00 a.m. to 5:00 p.m., Sunday 2:00 p.m. to 5:00 p.m, and weekends during December.

Woodstock also boasts an unusual museum—the **Vermont Raptor Center** at Vermont's Institute of Natural Science on Church Hill Road about 1½ miles from the Green. At the outdoor museum visitors can view over 25 species of New England hawks, owls, and eagles, including bald eagles and the great horned owl. All the birds are injured so that they cannot be released into the wild, but here the birds are protected and can be studied by those of us who might never have the opportunity to see them in their natural habitat. The center is open daily from 10:00 a.m. to 4:00 p.m.; closed Sundays during the winter months. Admission is $4 for adults, $1 for children 5 to 15.

Lodging
For those looking for the comfort of a country inn combined with resort amenities such as golf, tennis, and swimming, the **Woodstock Inn & Resort** right on the Green is the place to stay. Double rooms start at $135 per night. Call (802) 457-1100 or 800-448-7900 for reservations.

The **Lincoln Covered Bridge Inn** on US 4 in nearby West Woodstock is a 200-year-old farmhouse overlooking the Lincoln Covered Bridge and the Ottauquechee River. Double room rates including a full country breakfast run from $99 to $120. There is also a restaurant on the premises.

Call (802) 457-3312 for reservations. The **Kedron Valley Inn** on Route 106 in South Woodstock is known for its French cuisine and has accommodations with canopy beds and country patchwork quilts. Rooms range from $114 to $182 including breakfast (802-457-1473). The **Braeside Motel** on the east side of Woodstock offers accommodations at moderate prices (802-457-1366), and Rutland, about 40 minutes farther along US 4 west, has a much wider selection of reasonably priced lodging establishments.

Camping
The closest camping area to Woodstock is the state-operated **Quechee Recreation Area** near the Quechee Gorge. A trail runs from the camping area to the bottom of the gorge. Both tent and camper sites are available. For information, call (802) 295-2990.

Dining
Bentley's Restaurant, in Woodstock center (802-457-3232), serves dishes ranging from veal to Szechuan to fresh salads. Dinner entrées average about $15. Families may want to try **Spooner's Restaurant** in Spooner Barn on US 4 just east of Woodstock center. Spooner's has a children's menu, and specialties include western-style beef and traditional New England fare (802-457-4022). Prices are moderate.

For elegant dining, **The Prince and the Pauper** on Elm Street in Woodstock might please even royalty. The prix fixe menu ($28 per person) changes weekly, but dishes such as poached salmon and roast duckling are the norm. Call (802) 457-1818 for reservations.

Itinerary Options
For those with extra time, Day 10 is an excellent place for jumping off the itinerary to explore the Lakes Region of New Hampshire or to spend several days in northern Vermont, before continuing on to southern Vermont and the Berkshires.

The Lakes Region

To visit New Hampshire's largest lakes, Squam and
Winnipesaukee, continue south on Route 3, then east on
Route 104 after traveling through Franconia Notch State
Park. Weirs Beach is perhaps the most touristed spot on
Winnipesaukee, complete with a honky-tonk boardwalk
and the type of sandy beach normally found at seaside
resorts. Despite its touristy nature, Weirs Beach does have
beautiful views of the lake, and many excursion companies leave from there. **Mt. Washington Cruises** operates
three-hour boat cruises late May through late October and
Moonlight Dinner/Dance Cruises at night at the height of
the summer season. Day cruises cost about $12.50 for
adults, $6.25 for children. Dinner cruises are $26 to $32 per
person. Call (603) 366-5531 for departure times and tickets.

The **Winnipesaukee Railroad** runs lakeside scenic railroad trips in restored historic railroad cars. Excursions
leave from Weirs Beach and Meredith. Tickets that allow
you to get on and off the train as many times as you'd like
during the day are $7 for adults, $4.50 for children over 5.
The railroad operates on weekends only from Memorial
Day through late June, then daily through mid-October.
Call (603) 279-5253 for information.

Other Lakes Region attractions include **Annalee's
Doll Museum** in Meredith, **Castle in the Clouds** in
Moultonboro, the **Polar Caves** in Plymouth, and the slide
and surf coaster at Weirs Beach. There are numerous
accommodations and restaurants along Route 3 throughout the region.

Northern Vermont

Almost more than any other northeastern state, Vermont
embodies the spirit of New England many travelers hope
to discover when they visit this part of the world. Picture-
perfect town greens, winding river valleys, and the beautiful Green Mountains that turn gentle shades of pastel
colors at sunset all seem virtually unspoiled by modern
development. If you have extra time and wish to explore
this area more thoroughly, I suggest the following addition to your itinerary.

From the North Conway/Jackson area, travel south on Route 16 to Conway. At Conway, take the scenic Kancamagus Highway (Route 112) west to Interstate 93 north in Lincoln. I-93 will take you through Franconia Notch State Park, and you can visit the same sites (the Flume, the Old Man of the Mountains, the Ski Museum, etc.) as described in the main itinerary for Day 10, only you will come upon them in the opposite order.

Continue on I-93 north to St. Johnsbury, Vermont, then take US 2 west. Maple syrup lovers may want to visit the **Maple Grove Museum and Factory** on US 2 in St. Johnsbury. The museum is really just a small cottage where sugaring tools are displayed and a flat vat of syrup boils. Of more interest is the video on maple syrup making that plays continuously in the gift shop and the tour of the factory where maple candy is made. Visitors can tour the factory on weekdays year-round every 12 minutes from 8:00 a.m. to 11:45 a.m. and 12:30 p.m. to 4:15 p.m. for 75 cents.

From St. Johnsbury, travel on US 2 west only briefly, then take Route 15 west to Jeffersonville. At Jeffersonville, take Route 108 south through Smugglers Notch, past Mt. Mansfield and the Stowe ski area to the town of Stowe. At one point the road becomes very steep, narrow, and curvy but only for a short stretch. Alongside the road there are picnic areas and entrances to hiking trails.

Restaurants and accommodations are plentiful in Stowe—long a summer and winter resort—making it a good stopping place for the night. Perhaps the best-known hotel in Stowe is the **Trapp Family Lodge**, run by the Trapp family of "The Sound of Music" fame. With its chalet-style buildings bursting with flower boxes, and unrivaled views of Stowe below and the mountains beyond, the lodge easily lives up to its motto "a little of Austria . . . a lot of Vermont." During the summer there are outdoor evening concerts in the Trapp Family Meadow. Doubles range from $160 to $220 (802-253-8511 or 800-826-7000). The **Green Mountain Inn**, right in the heart of the village, is on the National Register of Historic Places. It is centrally located and more affordably priced at

$70 to $200. (802-253-7301 or 800-445-6629.) There is an excellent reservation service (800-24-STOWE) that can help book a room for you in your price range. In addition to some of the best skiing and hiking in New England, Stowe has good shopping, in-town recreational trails, an alpine slide at the mountain, and an auto toll road up Mt. Mansfield with outstanding views.

For a truly out of the ordinary experience, how about a llama trek into the mountains. **Northern Vermont Llama Company** operates half-day and full day treks (802-644-2257). The excursions leave from Smuggler's Notch just over the mountain from Stowe.

The next day head to Burlington (Vermont's largest city, although a small city by comparison to most) and Shelburne via Waterbury. Leaving Stowe take Route 100 south, which passes **Cold Hollow Cider Mill** and **Ben & Jerry's Ice Cream Factory**, both of which operate plant tours. Actually, there isn't much to see at Cold Hollow— the cider press and jelly kitchen aren't exactly exciting— but the cider samples are tasty, as are the other Vermont-made gourmet foods available for sampling and purchase. The Ben & Jerry's factory tour is fun for the whole family. Half of the $1 tour fee goes to charity, and the delectable ice cream samples fresh off the production line are well worth the other 50 cents.

From Waterbury, take US 89 northwest to Burlington. On the shores of Lake Champlain, it is home to the University of Vermont. Ferry rides across the lake to New York state are a pleasant way to see the lake and the Adirondack and Green mountains that surround it, but keep in mind you'll need to save at least a full afternoon or morning to visit the Shelburne Museum south of Burlington. If you do venture out on the lake, be sure to keep an eye out for "Champ," Lake Champlain's own fabled creature said to rival the Loch Ness monster. Ferries operate from Burlington late May through late October, and the crossing takes 1 hour each way. Call (802) 864-9804 for departure times and fares during your visit. (If you really want to extend your trip, Montreal, Canada, is only about two hours north of Burlington.)

From Burlington, travel on US 7 south to the **Shelburne Museum**, generally considered to have one of the best collections of early American antiques and folk art. The museum covers 45 acres and has 37 period homes housing its collection of art, china, silver, scrimshaw, Native American artifacts, carousel animals, decoys, weathervanes, ship figureheads, and antique toys and dolls. Some of the unique structures include a lighthouse, a round barn, a sidewheeler boat called the SS *Ticonderoga*, and a private railroad car. Built in the late 1800s, the latter has a plush interior of mahogany paneling, velvet upholstery, and modern bath and kitchen facilities.

Not to be missed is the hat and fragrance house, which contains much more than its name implies. Within its walls you'll find an especially fine assemblage of antique quilts, handwoven rugs, handmade lace, embroidered samplers, and costumes. The old-time country store, apothecary shop, and doctor's and dentist's offices in the general store building are fascinating; and the Electra Havemeyer Webb Memorial Building (built in memory of the woman philanthropist who founded the museum) has Degas, Manet, Rembrandt, and Monet originals. The museum is open from 10:00 a.m. to 5:00 p.m. daily from mid-May to mid-October. Admission (which will let you into the museum for two consecutive days) is $15 for adults, $6 for children 6 to 14.

After visiting the museum, you may wish to see nearby **Shelburne House and Farms** owned by Electra Havemeyer Webb's family. The estate, built in 1899, is stunningly set on Lake Champlain. Park architect Frederick Law Olmstead was consulted in the landscape design of the property. The estate now serves as an elegant inn open from late May through mid-October. Doubles range from $100 to $250 (802-985-8498 or 802-985-8686). Visitors can tour the farm daily beginning at 9:30 a.m., with the last tour leaving at 3:30 p.m., late May through mid-October. The farm makes its own delicious cheddar cheese that can be purchased at the farm store and visitor center. Proceeds go to the farm's nonprofit conservation education organization.

In addition to the Inn at Shelburne Farms, there are
numerous motels along US 7 between Shelburne and
Burlington. If you have time to travel one hour south to
Middlebury, I recommend staying there for the night, as it
will put you in better range for rejoining the main itinerary. Middlebury is a pleasant college town bisected by
Otter Creek Falls. **The Middlebury Inn** is the popular
place in town to stay (802-388-4961 or 800-842-4666).
Doubles are $80 to $144. The **Otter Creek Bakery** at 1
College Street has terrific breakfast pastries, bread sticks,
and picnic fixings.

From Middlebury, continue about one hour south on US
7 to Rutland. Follow the schedule for Day 11 from there,
beginning with a visit to Wilson Castle or the Vermont
Marble exhibit, then again south on US 7 to Manchester.

SOUTHERN VERMONT

This area of New England is particularly well traveled in autumn because of the abundant maple trees that turn brilliant orange and red as winter approaches. Southern Vermont's excellent ski resort, beautiful mountain vistas, and charming towns with their tidy village greens are reason enough to visit the region in any season.

Suggested Schedule

8:00 a.m.	Have breakfast, then leave Woodstock for Manchester. Visit the Marble Exhibit or Wilson Castle in Proctor on the way.
11:30 a.m.	Window-shop in Manchester Center and stroll along lovely Manchester Village's marble sidewalks.
1:00 p.m.	Lunch
2:00 p.m.	Visit Hildene.
4:00 p.m.	Take the Sky Line Drive to the top of Mt. Equinox, or if the weather refuses to cooperate, take your pick of the area's many other attractions.
6:00 p.m.	Check into a country inn for a memorable evening of fine dining and provincial comfort.

Travel Route: Woodstock to Manchester (64 miles)
From Woodstock, take US 4 to Rutland, passing by Killington and Pico ski areas, to connect with US 7. To visit either Wilson Castle or the Marble Exhibit travel on business US 4 past Rutland to West Proctor Road just past the junction with Route 3 north. Turn right onto West Proctor Road; the entrance to the castle is up about a mile on your left. The town of Proctor is five miles farther, and once there follow signs to the Marble Exhibit. After visiting these sites, backtrack to the junction of US 4 and US 7, and then take US 7 south from Rutland to Manchester Center. All along this highway there are views of the

Southern Vermont

Green Mountains on your left. Historic Manchester Village
is one mile from Manchester Center on Route 7A.

Manchester Center has an array of tidy shops inter-
spersed with Ralph Lauren and Liz Claiborne outlets,
among others. The Northshire Bookstore at the intersection of US 7 and Route 30 is one of the best bookstores in
New England and is definitely worth a visit. Orvis, the
mail order giant, has its flagship store on Route 7A in
Manchester. The Equinox Valley Nursery on Route 7A is
known for its colorful seasonal displays. The nursery's
annual fall pumpkin patch is especially festive.

The Chamber of Commerce, located on the Green as
you enter Manchester Center on US 7 traveling south, is
very helpful with sightseeing information. They're open
from 9:00 a.m. to 5:00 p.m. during the week, and from
10:00 a.m. to 4:00 p.m. on weekends. Hikers will want to

stop in at the U.S. Forest Service office on Route 30 just east of Manchester Center. They will furnish you with local hiking suggestions. Skiers will be pleased to know that both Stratton and Bromley mountains are convenient to the Manchester area. Bromley also operates an Alpine Ride during the summer months for $4.50.

Sightseeing Highlights

▲**Vermont Marble Exhibit**—Proctor, a small town about 8 miles from Rutland, calls itself the "marble capital of the world" because of the abundance of marble found in the area. At the Vermont Marble Exhibit on Main Street visitors have the chance to see a marble sculptor at work. There is also a film explaining the natural forces that created marble and the steps taken to mold this stone for artistic and functional purposes. You will see examples of Vermont marble throughout Proctor and, later in the day, as the sidewalks of Manchester Village. The exhibit is open daily mid-May through late October from 9:00 a.m. to 5:30 p.m., and there is an admission charge. During the winter, only the gift shop is open Monday through Saturday 9:00 a.m. to 4:00 p.m.

▲▲**Wilson Castle**—On West Proctor Road off Business US 4, west of Rutland about one-half mile from the Route 3 north turnoff, the nineteenth-century castle is set on 115 acres. Built by a Vermont doctor and his wealthy British wife, the castle is filled with an eclectic mix of European and Oriental pieces. Although the paint is peeling here and there, the hand-painted and hand-stenciled ceilings are unusual, and the colorful stained and etched glass windows throughout the house are quite beautiful. A Louis XV chair used by several popes, an ornate jewel case, an inlaid pool table, and a handsome curly maple fireplace in the master bedroom are a few of the other furnishings worth special note. The castle is open daily for guided tours from mid-May through late October from 9:00 a.m. to 6:00 p.m.; $6 for adults, $5.50 for seniors, $2 for children 6 to 12, children under 6 free.

▲**Southern Vermont Art Center**—The center is open from mid-May through October, Tuesday through Sunday.

(Also on July 4 and Columbus Day.) After viewing the changing exhibits by local artists, take a walk in the sculpture garden or on the botany trail, or have lunch in the attractive garden café where the menu changes daily. Lunch entrées are in the $8 range. Admission to the center is $3 for adults, 50 cents for students, children under 13 free. To get to the center, follow signs from Route 7A just south of Manchester Center.

▲▲**Hildene**—The stucco Georgian revival mansion just south of Manchester Village on Route 7A was built and owned by Robert Todd Lincoln, son of Abraham Lincoln. Hildene remained in the Lincoln family until 1975 and is now open to the public. The furnishings, including a 1,000-pipe player organ complete with over 240 rolls of music and a stove-pipe hat worn by the president, belonged to the Lincolns. Beautifully set in the Manchester valley, Hildene's expansive front lawn was used as a driving range by avid golfer Robert Todd Lincoln. The estate's formal English-style gardens were designed by his daughter, Jesse, after she returned from England. Many special events such as polo, symphony concerts, sleigh rides, and cross-country skiing take place on the estate's "meadow-lands." Even though the home is only open for tours from May through October, you may want to call (802) 362-1788 to see if there are any special goings-on should your visit happen to fall in the off-season. Christmas candlelight tours are especially popular. Admission to the house is $6 for adults, $3 for children 6 to 14, children under 6 are free. The last tour of the day leaves at 4:00 p.m.

▲**Norman Rockwell Exhibition and Gift Shop**—More a gift shop than a museum, this place on 7A in Arlington has hundreds of Rockwell magazine covers on display but no original work. There is a film presentation on the artist. Admission is $1, and the shop is open daily from 9:00 a.m. to 5:00 p.m. May through October and from 10:00 a.m. to 4:00 p.m. during the rest of the year. I prefer the Rockwell Museum in Stockbridge, Massachusetts, which you can visit two days hence.

▲**Sky Line Drive**—For better views of the Green
Mountains, take the 5.2-mile-long Sky Line Drive (toll
road) to the top of Mt. Equinox, the highest peak in the
Taconic range. The drive is well worth taking on a clear
day and is particularly dramatic at the height of fall
foliage. There are a number of picnic areas and hiking
trails on the way up and an inn at the 3,835-foot summit,
but despite the view, you're better off opting for accommodations down in the village. The toll is $6 per car, and
the drive is open from 8:00 a.m. to 10:00 p.m. daily, May 1
to November 1. Entrance to the auto road is on Route 7A
south of Manchester Village.

Lodging and Dining
Reservations for the Manchester area are strongly advised,
especially on weekends and during leaf-peeping season.
At the Equinox, for example, rooms are often completely
booked as much as six months in advance for peak
foliage weekends. Some lodging establishments do have
minimum stay requirements of two nights or more during
high season, so be sure to check ahead of time. If the
lodgings listed below are full during your visit, you may
want to contact Manchester and the Mountains Area
Lodgings (800-677-STAY). They will try to locate a room
for you in your price range, and there is no charge for
the service.

The majestic **Equinox Hotel Resort and Spa** reigns
supreme over historic Manchester Village. The historic
hotel has recently been renovated and now serves as a
full-service resort and spa. The grand exterior appears to
stretch endlessly, as do the marble sidewalks that surround the building. Carriage rides are available from the
hotel's doorstep. Rooms in season will run over $150 per
night for two including breakfast. For extra pampering,
you may want to make use of the resort's spa facilities.
Call (802) 362-4700 or (800) 362-4747 for reservations.
Dinner entrées in the hotel's main dining room range from
$16 to $24, with "lighter entrées" (really expanded portions of appetizers) ranging from $8.25 to $12.75. **Marsh
Tavern** at the hotel has a buffet luncheon, dinner entrées

from hamburgers to basil linguini ($8.95–$15), and
evening entertainment.

The **Reluctant Panther** on West Road right in
Manchester Village (802-362-2568 or 800-822-2331) has
pleasing lodging and dining facilities. Room rates are
based on a modified American Plan and range from $170
to $295. The inn's restaurant features hearty soups, stews,
and pies in the winter and lighter fare such as seafood
and grilled dishes during the summer.

The **1811 House** (802-362-1811 or 800-432-1811), also
in the village center, became an inn in 1811 but was built
in the 1770s. Authentically furnished with fine antiques,
the house is on the National Register of Historic Places
and once belonged to Mary Lincoln Isham, President
Lincoln's granddaughter. Doubles run from $110 to $180
including a full breakfast (a two-night minimum stay is
required on weekends, during fall foliage, and on holidays). There is a pub on the premises (open from 5:00
p.m. to 7:30 p.m.). The **Inn at Manchester,** just down the
street on Route 7A toward Manchester Center, is open all
year and serves a complete breakfast. Rates range from
$65 to $130. Call (802) 362-1793 for reservations. The **Seth
Warner Inn** (802) 362-3830 also on 7A, has sunny rooms
with country furnishings ($85 for two including breakfast).

For more of a retreat, try the **Birch Hill Inn**, exquisitely
set in the Vermont countryside several miles from town on
West Road. The inn has a private trout pond and outdoor
swimming pool. The hosts and guests dine together on
Monday, Tuesday, Friday, and Saturday evenings. Main
courses such as veal marsala, pork tenderloin, chicken
parmesan, cornish game hens, and beefalo specialties
(made with the hybrid cow-buffalo cross bred at the farm
next door) are always accompanied by soup, two vegeta-
bles, a potato or rice dish, wine, and dessert. Accommodations start at $49 per person including breakfast (dinner
is extra). Call (802) 362-2761 for reservations.

There are many motels in the vicinity of Manchester.
Most of them are located on the outskirts of town on
Routes 30, 7, and 7A. One of the nicest is the **North
Shire** on 7A on the south side of the village. Rooms are

spacious and attractively furnished and have lovely mountain views. The outdoor pool is pleasant, as are the helpful hosts who are more than willing to provide you with sightseeing and dining suggestions. Doubles are $65 to $79 per day including continental breakfast in peak season (802-362-2336).

If your lodging establishment doesn't serve food, the Manchester area has plenty of restaurants to satisfy just about any food craving. For breakfast, try **Up For Breakfast** on Main Street in Manchester Center, where breakfast dishes are far from ordinary. Or indulge in pancakes at the **Pancake House** just south of the Route 7/Route 30 junction. The **Park Bench**, also on Route 7, is nearby and is popular for lunch. **Christo's** next to Up for Breakfast features pizza and pasta at moderate prices. For dessert, the aroma from the **Cookie House** is hard to resist, while Vermont's own **Ben & Jerry's** ice cream shop just a couple of doors away will not do much to thin one's waistline either. **The Black Swan** (802-362-3807) on Route 7 between Manchester Center and the historic Village is renowned for fine dining, as is the **Arlington Inn** (802-375-6532) on Route 7A in nearby Arlington.

If you want to ship home some of Vermont's celebrated cheddar cheese, the Grand Union supermarket in Manchester Center is one of the best place in the area to purchase it. They have the cheese already packed for shipping, and their prices tend to be lower than elsewhere. The supermarket is also a good place to purchase Vermont maple syrup and prepared salads for picnicking.

Camping

Emerald Lake State Park, in East Dorset about 8 miles north of Manchester Center on US 7, has camping, swimming, a nature trail, and boating on a beautiful green lake that lives up to its name. The camping area has 105 sites, no hookups, 35 lean-tos, bathrooms, and pay showers. Canoes and rowboats can be rented for an outing on the lake. Call (802) 362-1655 for reservations.

Camping on the Battenkill is a private campground with both tent and RV sites, plus swimming and fishing on

the Battenkill River. The campground, located on Route
7A in Arlington, is open from mid-April through October.
The rate is $15 per campsite. Call (802) 375-6663 for
reservations.

Nightlife
During June, July, and August, one can enjoy summer
stock productions at the **Dorset Playhouse** on Route 30
5 miles north of Manchester Center. Call (802) 867-5777
for ticket information.

Itinerary Options
The Battenkill River, running from Manchester southwest
through Arlington, is frequented by canoeists. **Battenkill
Canoe Ltd.** at 1 River Road in Arlington can outfit you
with the canoe trip of your choice. Contact them at (802)
362-2800 for additional information.

    Battenkill Sports Bicycle Shop at the junction of
Routes 7 and 30 in Manchester Center can fix you up with
a mountain or touring bike for exploring the beautiful surrounding countryside. Call (802) 362-2734 or (800) 421-
5628 for rental information.

    Lake George, New York, a very popular lake resort, is
only 43 miles from Rutland. To get there, continue on US
4 west from Rutland to Fort Ann. Then take Route 149
west to US 9 and follow it north to the town of Lake
George.

    Fort Ticonderoga, about 50 miles northwest of Rutland
at Ticonderoga, New York, is also a popular tourist destination. To get to the fort, continue on US 4 west at
Rutland to Whitehall, then take Route 22 north to
Ticonderoga. The fort is open daily from mid-May through
mid-October from 9:00 a.m. to 5:00 p.m., until 6:00 p.m.
during July and August. Admission is $6 for adults, $4 for
children 10 to 13, children under 10 free.

BENNINGTON AND THE BERKSHIRES

Bennington, Vermont, was the site of a major Revolutionary War victory for the colonists in 1777. Today, looking
at Old Bennington's graceful homes, it is hard to believe
that a war ever took place there.

Suggested Schedule

8:00 a.m.	Breakfast.
9:00 a.m.	Travel to Bennington and visit the Bennington Monument and Museum.
12:00 noon	Leave for Williamstown, Massachusetts.
12:30 p.m.	Lunch in Williamstown.
1:30 p.m.	Spend the afternoon exploring the Clark Institute and the Williams College art museum.
6:00 p.m.	Check into your Berkshire accommodation, your home base for the next two nights.

Travel Route: Manchester to Stockbridge/Lenox (75 miles)

From the Manchester area, continue on Route 7A south to
Bennington. Covered bridge enthusiasts should make a
short detour at Arlington to Route 313 where there are
covered bridges on both sides of 7A. Farther along Route
7A, take Route 67 west at South Shaftsbury to Route 67A
in North Bennington. There are two more covered bridges
in quick succession along Route 67A as you approach Old
Bennington.

Within Bennington itself, driving is confusing because
roads are not well-marked and route signs seem to contra-
dict one another. The easiest way to get your bearings is
to look for the Bennington Monument, which stands high
on the hill above the town, and drive toward it. At the
monument, ask directions to the museum.

Leaving Bennington, take US 7 south, stopping in
Williamstown for the afternoon, then continue on US 7 to
Lenox and Stockbridge in the heart of the Berkshire region

Bennington Sightseeing Highlights

▲▲**The Bennington Museum**—The primary reason for
visiting this museum, approximately one-half mile from
the Bennington Monument on Route 9, is its collection of
works by famed American folk artist Grandma Moses,
who started to paint in her seventies and continued to be
productive well into her nineties. The museum's collection
also includes early American furniture, glassware, pottery,
military artifacts, and household items such as pedal-
operated sewing machines. The museum is open daily
from 9:00 a.m. to 5:00 p.m. March 1 through November
except for Thanksgiving Day. Call (802) 447-1571 for
hours during the rest of the year. Admission is $5 for
adults, $3.50 for students and senior citizens, children
under 12 are free. Family admission for two adults and
two children under 18 is $10.

▲**The Bennington Monument**—Completed in 1891, the
monument commemorates the Battle of Bennington and is
the centerpiece of lovely Old Bennington. It warrants a
visit on any clear day for the view, and it is a must at the
height of fall foliage season. You can see three states—
Massachusetts, New York, and Vermont—from the observation deck. An elevator takes you to the top of the 306-
foot structure, so there is no stair-climbing involved. A
small admission fee is charged. The well-groomed houses
that line the road leading to and from the monument are
worth a look as well. The monument is open daily April
through October from 9:00 a.m. to 5:00 p.m. Admission is
$1 for adults, 50 cents for children.

▲**The Old First Church**—Adjacent to the Town Green
in Old Bennington, this is a lovely example of early
nineteenth-century church architecture in New England.
Perhaps more interesting, though, is its graveyard with
headstones dating back to the Revolutionary War. Poet
Robert Frost is buried here.

▲**Park-McCullough House**—If you have time, you may
want to visit this lovely 35-room Victorian mansion in
North Bennington. Once home to two Vermont governors,
the house is filled with family antiques and beautiful
details such as a stained-glass skylight and intricately pat-

terned frosted-glass light fixtures. The house is open for
tours from early May through October 10:00 a.m.
to 4:00 p.m., with the last tour leaving at 3:00 p.m.
Admission is $4 for adults, $2.50 for seniors, $1.50 for
youths 12 to 17. Special "Victorian Christmas" tours
are run during the holidays. Call (802) 442-5441 for
a schedule.

Williamstown Sightseeing Highlights
In this quintessential college town, Williams College dominates just about every aspect of town life, providing the
residents of this sleepy Berkshire community with a
wealth of cultural activities that many rural communities
lack, including two outstanding art museums.
▲▲▲**Sterling & Francine Clark Art Institute**—The
museum has room after room of stunning French impressionist paintings, Renoir and Monet among others, and
works by noted American painters such as Homer, Cassatt,
and Sargent. The fine collection also includes English
silver and works dating back to the fifteenth century.
Admission is free. Open 10:00 a.m. to 5:00 p.m. Tuesday
through Sunday. Closed on Thanksgiving, Christmas, and
New Year's Day. The museum is open Memorial, Labor,
and Columbus days.
▲▲**Williams College Art Museum**—The museum's
collection ranges from ancient Greek vases to Andy
Warhol pop art. There is also a gallery devoted to the
artist brothers, Maurice and Charles Prendergast. Admission is free. Open 10:00 a.m. to 5:00 p.m. Monday through
Saturday, and Sunday from 1:00 to 5:00 p.m. The museum
is closed for Thanksgiving, Christmas, and New Year's Day.
▲**The Williamstown Theatre Festival**—The festival is
widely known for its high-quality summer productions.
Many popular actors got their start here, and some return
on occasion to hone their stage skills. Call (413) 597-3400
for performance and ticket information.

Lodging and Dining
You can find comfortable lodging at the **Williams Inn**
(413-458-9371) on the Green in Williamstown if you plan

to stay for a performance at the playhouse. If you're not attending the theater, I suggest putting up for the next two nights in Stockbridge or Lenox, both better jumping-off points for Berkshire activities.

The Red Lion Inn in Stockbridge is one of the best-known inns in the area and deservedly so. The Red Lion, the focal point of the town, has been treating its guests regally for over 200 years. Double rooms at the inn start around $100 in peak season (May through October). Singles and two-room suites are also available. Call (413) 298-5545 for reservations. If you are unable to book a room here, at least partake of a traditional New England meal such as prime rib, stuffed lobster, or scrod in the main dining room; or people-watch while sipping cocktails on the inn's front porch. The **Lion's Den** downstairs has pub fare and entertainment in the evenings.

There are two pleasant inns in the quiet town of South Lee, once a mill town, about a mile and a half from Stockbridge. The **Merrell Tavern Inn**, built in 1794, has the only remaining colonial circular bar in America. Rooms are furnished with antiques, and the property borders on the Housatonic River. Double rooms including an ample breakfast range from $65 to $135 per night (413-243-1794). Just across the street, the **Federal House**, known locally for its fine European cuisine, also rents rooms to overnight guests. Call (413) 243-1824 for dining or lodging reservations.

Lovely Lenox has its share of attractive inns right in the center of town on Walker Street. Each guest room in the **Walker House** is named after a famous composer and is furnished accordingly. Guests are welcome to use the inn's delightful porches or watch movies in the library. The hosts are warm and friendly, and breakfast and afternoon tea are included in the room rates of $70 to $150 (413-637-1271). The **Gables Inn** just down the street was once the home of Edith Wharton. Rooms here are also thematic—the Shakespeare room, the Show Business room, and the Presidential room with pictures and memorabilia of past presidents. Rates, including continental breakfast at an elegantly set table, are $60 to $195 per night depending on the season and type of room. There's also a pool on the premises. Call (413) 637-3416.

Two other inns on Walker Street have restaurants and overnight accommodations. **Gateways Inn and Restaurant** has four large suites with private baths, fireplaces, and curly maple furniture for $90 to $295 (413-637-2532). Prix fixe dinners at $19.50 per person feature dishes such as breast of chicken topped with crawfish, truffle and crêpes served in a honey liqueur sauce, and medallions of monkfish stuffed with Norwegian salmon and topped with a fresh basil sauce. The menu at the **Candlelight Inn** changes seasonally but is primarily continental and American in focus. Dinner entrées range from $17.95 to $24.95, and lunch generally runs $4.95 to $14.95. Try the Chocolate Chippie for dessert. Upstairs rooms range from $90 to $155 per night in season and $65 to $120 per night in the off-season (413-637-1555).

Outside Lenox, a turreted estate has been turned into one of the most elegant lodging establishments around. Set on 85 acres, and restored by the owners of the Red Lion Inn, **Blantyre** is truly a feast for the eyes. You'll have to have a deep pocketbook to stay there, however, as rooms average about $250 per night—tennis and continental breakfast included. Call (413) 637-3556 for reservations.

Somewhat more affordable are the strip of motels on US 7 between Pittsfield and Lenox, including the **Suisse Chalet** where a double room goes for $40 to $65 a night (413-637-3560 or 1-800-5-CHALET). More motels can also be found on US 7 between Stockbridge and Great Barrington. The area abounds with country inns, but accommodations do fill up quickly on weekends so you may want to call the Berkshire Visitor's Bureau at (413) 443-9186 for a complete lodging list.

For less formal dining options than listed above, **Michael's** on Elm Street in Stockbridge serves a variety of American dishes, with dinner prices ranging from $7 to $16. For gourmet takeout or eat-in pasta salads, try **La Fete Chez Vous** down an alley off Main Street between the Red Lion and Elm Street. **The Cafe** in the mews

The Berkshires

behind the Red Lion also serves salads and sandwiches
for about $5.

Camping
The **Pittsfield State Forest** (413-442-8992) has 31 campsites ($8 to $10), and **October Mountain State Forest**
(413-243-1778) in Lee has 50. The campground at October
Mountain is more convenient for sightseeing, so reservations are strongly recommended. Sites are about $12 per
night. Both campgrounds have bathrooms with wheelchair
access and are open seasonally. **Bonnie Brae Cabins**

and Campsites at Pontoosuc Lake just off US 7 several
miles north of downtown Pittsfield might also be an economical alternative to staying in a country inn. Open May
through mid-October, Bonnie Brae has cabins that rent for
$35 to $55 per night, and campsites go for about $20 per
night. Call (413) 442-3754 for information.

Itinerary Options

If you would prefer to spend your day outdoors, take the
scenic drive over Mt. Greylock. On fair days the view of
the Berkshires is extraordinary. The entrance to the visitors center is off US 7 just south of New Ashford.

Horse-racing fans traveling this route in August may
want to take a 35-mile detour from Arlington, Vermont, to
Saratoga Springs, New York. In addition to being recog-
nized for thoroughbred horse-racing and natural springs,
Saratoga also has fine homes in its favor. The **National
Museum of Racing and Thoroughbred Hall of Fame**
is in Saratoga, as well as the unusual **Petrified Sea
Gardens**.

Historic Deerfield

Deerfield, about 35 miles southeast of Williamstown,
Massachusetts, is one of the most perfectly preserved historic towns in New England. While many of the buildings
are privately owned by either individuals or Deerfield
Academy, twelve of them are open to the public and can
be toured with one admission ticket. Guided tours of the
houses last thirty minutes each, so you'll need a full day if
you want to visit them all. Tickets are $10 for adults, $5
for children 6 to 17, and can be purchased at the information center on the village's main street (called The Street).
The buildings are open daily from 9:30 a.m. to 4:30 p.m.
except Thanksgiving, Christmas Eve, and Christmas.

In addition to the historic houses, the **Memorial Hall
Museum** on Memorial Street in the center of Deerfield has
period rooms including a Victorian bedroom and a colonial kitchen. Indian artifacts and pottery, handmade quilts,
and nineteenth-century clothing are also on display. The
museum is open weekdays from 10:00 a.m. to 4:30 p.m.,

Saturday and Sunday from 12:30 p.m. to 4:30 p.m. May 1 through October 31. Admission is $3 for adults, $1.50 for students, 75 cents for children 6 to 12. The grounds of lovely Deerfield Academy are also worth strolling through.

If you do plan to stay at Deerfield for the day, there are picnic tables behind the information center. The **Deerfield Inn** right across the street from the information center is a fine lodging and dining establishment. Lunch entrées such as shrimp scampi, oriental chicken, and seafood casserole range from $8.75 to $10.25. Pheasant, veal with wild mushrooms, and venison dishes are just a sampling of the varied dinner menu, priced from $17 to $23. Overnight accommodations including breakfast start at $61 per person. Call (413) 774-5587 for reservations.

To get to Deerfield, take Route 2 east from Williams-town to Greenfield. From Greenfield, follow US 5 south to Deerfield.

THE BERKSHIRES

Because the Berkshires offer the visitor so much in the way of outdoor recreation, such as golf, skiing, and hiking, cultural events such as the Boston Symphony Orchestra at Tanglewood, picturesque villages such as Stockbridge, and of course the beauty of the Berkshire hills themselves, the area has been a popular resort for over a hundred years. Couple the attractions with the fact that the Berkshires are only three hours from both New York City and Boston, and it is amazing that the area is not overrun with souvenir shop malls, factory outlets, and T-shirt shops designed to take advantage of the tourist dollar. Fortunately, due to careful planning, most towns remain much as they were when Norman Rockwell painted here in the 1950s, and many have changed little in the last century.

Suggested Schedule

9:00 a.m.	Breakfast.
10:00 a.m.	Visit Hancock Shaker Village.
12:30 p.m.	Lunch.
1:30 p.m.	Tour Chesterwood.
3:30 p.m.	Visit the Norman Rockwell Museum.
4:30 p.m.	Stroll down Main Street in Stockbridge, perhaps stopping at the Red Lion for tea or a cocktail and people-watching.
6:00 p.m.	Dinner.
8:00 p.m.	Take in an evening performance of the entertainment of your choice.

Travel Route

Travel to Hancock Shaker Village at the junction of US 20 and Route 41 about 12 miles northwest of Stockbridge. From the village you'll take Route 41 south to Route 102 east, following it until it intersects with Route 183 south. Take Route 183 south and follow signs to Chesterwood. After leaving Chesterwood, retrace your steps back to

Route 102, and continue on Route 102 east for 2 miles into Stockbridge Center. The tourist information booth on Main Street in Stockbridge can provide you with directions to other area points of interest, and in most cases, sights are well marked by directional signs.

Sightseeing Highlights
▲▲▲**Hancock Shaker Village**—Allow at least two hours to explore this village, one of the best examples of the everyday life of an unusual religious sect called the Shakers. There are live demonstrations of Shaker crafts such as broom making and basket weaving. Two 60-minute tours daily at 10:30 a.m. and 2:00 p.m. take you through part of the village. If you are unable to time your visit for a guided tour, you are free to tour the complex on your own. The descriptive panels in each room describe different aspects of Shaker life. Don't miss the unique round barn. The village is open daily from April through November. The hours are 9:30 a.m. to 5:00 p.m. Memorial Day weekend through October, 10:00 a.m. to 3:00 p.m. during April, May, and November. The village is located at the junction of Routes 41 and 20 in Hancock. There are picnic tables outside the visitor center. Entrance fees are $9 for adults, $8 for students and seniors, $4.50 for children 6 to 12, and $25 for families. For a truly unusual evening, visit the village for a candlelight Shaker dinner and tour. You'll tour the village and then dine on traditional Shaker dishes while seated communal style at one of the long tables in the "Believers Room." The dinner events usually begin at 5:00 p.m. on Saturday evenings during the summer and early fall, and run about $35 per person. Call (413) 443-0188 for reservations.
▲▲**Chesterwood**—This was the summer home of sculptor Daniel Chester French, who is known for the Lincoln Memorial in Washington and the Minute Man statue in Concord, Massachusetts, as well as many other works that adorn governmental buildings. Plaster castings of his works are displayed in his barn, home, and studio. Many of his works were so large he had to transport them out of his studio on railroad tracks just to see how they'd look

in the sunlight. Each summer, usually beginning July 4th weekend, contemporary sculpture from local artists is on exhibit throughout the grounds and along the nature trail. Other annual events include an antique show in May, a flower show in July, and Christmas at Chesterwood. The museum is operated by the National Trust and is open daily May through October from 10:00 a.m. to 5:00 p.m. There is a picnic area next to the parking lot. Admission is $5.50 for adults, $3 for children ages 13 to 18, and $1 for children ages 7 to 12.

▲▲**The Norman Rockwell Museum**—In 1993 the museum moved from its previous quarters in the quaint "Old Corner House" on Main Street in downtown Stockbridge to this 4.4 million-dollar facility just west of town. Now the museum can display up to one third of its over 500 Rockwell works at a time, and exhibits also include the venerated artist's studio. Devoted Rockwell fans will enjoy this choice collection, and those previously indifferent to Rockwell will become converts when they witness first-hand the clarity and vitality of his oils. Open daily from 10:00 a.m. to 5:00 p.m. May through October. November through April the museum is open Monday through Friday from 11:00 a.m. to 4:00 p.m., and on Saturday and Sunday from 10:00 a.m. to 5:00 p.m. It is closed on Christmas, Thanksgiving, and New Year's Day, and for ten days in January. Admission is $8 for adults, $2 for children 6 to 18.

▲**The Berkshire Botanical Garden**—This 15-acre botanic garden off Route 102, just before you come to the intersection of Route 183, is a nice spot for a picnic lunch between visits to Hancock Shaker Village and Chesterwood. The center is open daily from 10:00 a.m. to 5:00 p.m. The greenhouses are open year-round, while the gardens may be toured mid-May through October, and admission is charged during those months (somewhat pricey for a botanic garden of this size, the garden is run by a non-profit organization). Admission is $5 for adults, $4 for seniors, $1 for children 6 to 12, and $10 for a family.

▲**Naumkeag**—Designed by Stanford White, this stately brick and shingle home open to the public is about one-

half mile from the Red Lion Inn on Prospect Hill Road.
The formal gardens are open from 10:00 a.m. to 5:00 p.m.
during the summer. The house may be toured Tuesday
through Sunday beginning at 10:00 a.m. with the last tour
leaving at 4:15 p.m. Admission to the house and gardens
is $6, admission to the house or garden alone is $4. Open
daily Memorial Day through Labor Day, on weekends and
holidays from Labor Day through Columbus Day.

▲**The Mount**—Off US 7 between Lenox and Stockbridge,
this was the summer estate of American novelist Edith
Wharton. *Ethan Frome*, perhaps her most famous novel,
was set in Lenox. Visitors can tour the property during the
summer months. Admission is $4.50 for adults, $4 for
seniors, and $2.50 for children ages 13 to 18. Plays based
on the author's works are presented here during July and
August. Tickets to the matinee performances include afternoon tea. Call (413) 637-1899 for complete details.

▲**Arrowhead**—Author Herman Melville made his home
here for thirteen years during the mid-1800s. See the
room where Melville penned *Moby Dick* and several other
novels. Located on Holmes Road in Pittsfield, Arrowhead
is open for guided tours Memorial Day through October.
The hours are 10:00 a.m. to 4:30 p.m. Monday through
Saturday, and Sunday from 11:00 a.m. to 3:30 p.m.
After Labor Day the museum is closed on Tuesday and
Wednesday. Admission is $3.50 for adults, $3 for seniors,
and $2 for children 6 to 16.

▲**The Berkshire Museum**—The museum is a combination art and natural history museum. Its collections include
everything from gemstones to piranhas to boa constrictors
to a fine selection of landscapes by artists of the Hudson
River School. Located at 39 South Street on US 7 in
Pittsfield, the museum is open Tuesday through Saturday
from 10:00 a.m. to 5:00 p.m., and Sunday from 1:00 p.m.
to 5:00 p.m. During July and August, it is also open on
Monday from 10:00 a.m. to 5:00 p.m. Admission is $3 for
adults, $2 for students and seniors, and $1 for children
12 to 18.

Other Sights—There are several historic homes in
Stockbridge that visitors can tour during the summer

months. The **Mission House Museum** on West Main Street in Stockbridge was built in 1739 for the Reverend John Sargeant, the first Christian missionary to the Stockbridge Indians. The house originally stood on the hill overlooking town but was moved to its present location in 1926. Tours of the house and garden run Tuesday through Sunday from 11:00 a.m. to 4:00 p.m. Memorial Day weekend through Columbus Day. Admission is $4 for adults, $1 for children 6 to 12. Diagonally across the street is the **Merwin House**, which can be toured June 1 through October 15 on Tuesday, Thursday, Saturday, and Sunday from 12:00 to 5:00 p.m. Admission is $4 for adults and $2 for children.

Train buffs may wish to visit the **Berkshire Scenic Railway Museum** in Lenox. Call (413) 637-2210 for ticket and schedule information if you're interested in taking the train ride along the Housatonic River. The museum is open from 10:00 a.m. to 3:00 p.m. weekends and holidays June through October. Admission is free.

In Great Barrington, south of Stockbridge, the **Albert Schweitzer Center** is a museum and library dedicated to Dr. Schweitzer. There is a wildlife sanctuary on the grounds. The center is open Tuesday through Saturday from 10:00 a.m. to 4:00 p.m., and Sunday from noon to 4:00 p.m. during the summer, and on weekends from 11:00 a.m. to 4:00 p.m. during the winter months. Donations are requested.

Performing Arts

A visit to **Tanglewood**, the Boston Symphony Orchestra's summer home in Lenox, is the favorite form of nighttime entertainment in the Berkshires. The BSO performs in the "Shed" on lovely wooded grounds. Tickets are available for seating in the Shed, but on clear nights Beethoven is best heard with a champagne picnic on the lawn. Bring your own blanket and dress warmly. Early birds can catch afternoon rehearsal performances at bargain prices. Call the box office at (413) 637-1940 for information during the summer months. In the off-season, you'll need to contact the BSO's office in Boston, (617) 266-1492, for details.

Tanglewood is located off Route 183 about two miles
south of Lenox Center.

Jacob's Pillow is also a popular summer cultural event
The dance festival features various well-known and tal-
ented traveling dance troupes. The Pillow is located in
Becket on US 20 about eight miles from Lee. Call (413)
243-0745 for schedule and tickets.

Other cultural events in the area include the **Berkshire
Theatre Festival** in Stockbridge (413-298-5576), the
Berkshire Ballet in Pittsfield (413-442-1307), the
Berkshire Opera Company (413-243-1343), and the
Berkshire Public Theatre in Pittsfield (413-445-4631).

The **Berkshire Ticket Booth** at the Chamber Office in
the Lenox Academy building at 75 Main Street in Lenox
sells tickets to area events. The booth is open Monday
through Saturday from 1:00 to 5:00 p.m.; it sells same-day
discounted tickets whenever they are available.

Itinerary Option
From the Berkshires, it is only a 2-hour drive to the
Catskill mountains in New York state. The Catskills are
somewhat less traveled during fall foliage than most of
New England, but the scenery is no less spectacular. To
get there, follow US 7 south to Great Barrington. From
Great Barrington, follow Route 23 west to Hudson, New
York. At Hudson, cross the Rip Van Winkle Bridge to
Catskill, New York.

CONNECTICUT RIVER VALLEY

Leaving the Berkshires behind, you'll be exposed to a castle, a capital, and culture as you travel along the Connecticut River today.

Suggested Schedule

8:00 a.m.	Have breakfast and leave the Berkshires.
10:30 a.m.	Tour Nook Farm.
12:30 p.m.	Lunch in Hartford or picnic along the Connecticut River.
2:30 p.m.	Visit Gillette's Castle.
4:00 p.m.	Amble along Essex's Main Street.
5:00 p.m.	Have an early dinner or late afternoon snack at the Griswold Inn.
6:00 p.m.	Head on up the coast to settle in for the night in Mystic.

Travel Route: Stockbridge to Mystic (110 miles)
From Stockbridge, head south on US 7 through the antique-lovers' havens of South Egremont and Sheffield. (Nature lovers with extra time may want to stop at **Bartholomew's Cobble**, a delightful 277-acre nature preserve off of route 7A south of Sheffield.) At Canaan, take US 44 east. After entering West Hartford, turn right onto Prospect. Then after about five minutes, turn left on Farmington Avenue. The parking lot for the Stowe and Twain houses is on your right immediately after the Woodland Street stoplight.

Alternative Route to Hartford: If you have extra time, a more scenic route from the Berkshires to Hartford is through the northwestern corner of Connecticut, which many consider the prettiest part of the state. Instead of turning east at Canaan, continue on US 7 south to Kent, passing through West Cornwall where there is a covered bridge. From Kent, take Route 341 east through Warren to Woodville. At Woodville, go east on US 202 to Litchfield, a showplace for exquisite eighteenth-century estates. The

Congregational church on Litchfield's village green is widely noted for its classic New England architecture. Leaving Litchfield, take Route 118 east to Route 4, then follow 4 east to West Hartford. Art lovers following this alternate route should visit the **Hill-Stead Museum** in Farmington, originally designed as a private home by architect Stanford White. The house is now filled with choice furnishings and impressionist paintings, and the gardens and grounds are lovely. Call (203) 677-4787 for hours of operation. The museum is closed from mid-January to mid-February. Admission is $5 for adults, $4 for seniors and students, and $2 for children under 12.

From Hartford, take Interstate 84 east to Interstate 91 south. Exit I-91 south at Route 9 south and pass by Middletown, home of Wesleyan University. At Exit 10 take Route 154 south. A good place to picnic is Haddam Meadows State Park right along the river just off this highway. To visit the Goodspeed Opera House and Gillette's Castle, take Route 82 east and follow signs to both.

After conquering the castle, retrace your steps to Route 154 south to get to Essex, an attractive town whose past and present have been shaped by nautical endeavors. In

1814, during the War of 1812, the British raided Essex and burned many of the town's ships, causing great hardship to the townspeople. Today, well-kept houses are discreetly tucked away on the waterfront, while the marina is filled with pleasure craft. From Essex, take Route 154 south to the intersection with Route 9, then take Route 9 south to Interstate 95 north, getting off at the Mystic Exit, #90 (Route 27).

Sightseeing Highlights

▲▲▲**Nook Farm**—Only a handful of houses remain from this nineteenth-century community for the literary elite of Hartford. Two are open to the public and worth seeing: the homes of Harriet Beecher Stowe and Samuel Clemens (Mark Twain). The Beecher Stowe house exemplifies a conventional upper-middle-class Victorian home, whereas the more pretentious Twain house is a monument to his eccentricities. In both cases, many of the writers' personal effects have been preserved, among them, Stowe's original paintings and Twain's bed and the dining room chair from which he told fantastic tales to his guests and family. Tour guides recount humorous details from the authors' everyday lives. The guided tour of both homes takes approximately an hour and fifteen minutes. Admission is charged. Nook Farm is open June 1 through Columbus Day, and the month of December, Monday through Saturday from 9:30 a.m. to 4:00 p.m., Sunday from noon to 4:00 p.m. Hours the rest of the year are 9:30 a.m. to 4:00 p.m. Tuesday through Saturday, and 12:00 p.m. to 4:00 p.m. on Sunday. Admission is $10 for adults and $4.50 for children under 16. If you're ready for lunch after Nook Farm, drive one mile into Hartford's center. The best selection of restaurants is found along Main Street.

Goodspeed's Opera House—Somewhat of an area landmark, this attractive building on the banks of the Connecticut River in East Haddam will catch your eye on the way to Gillette's Castle. Tours are available for $1 for adults and 50 cents for children. Should you decide to stay in the area awhile, the opera house hosts evening performances of popular musicals April through December. You

can picnic on the river's edge prior to a show. Call (203)
873-8668 for schedule and ticket information.

▲▲**Gillette's Castle**—They say a man's home is his
castle, and in actor William Gillette's case, that statement
can be taken literally. Best known for his portrayal of
Sherlock Holmes, Gillette built his castle overlooking
the Connecticut River in Hadlyme. The jagged stone exterior is striking, but except for several intricately carved
wooden doors, the interior is fairly modest. Children will
no doubt enjoy exploring the castle, and theater buffs
will appreciate the Broadway memorabilia on display.
Admission, $2 for adults and $1 for children 6 to 11, is
reasonable and won't break the family pocketbook. The
castle grounds are a Connecticut state park, so there are
picnic tables available as well as a souvenir shop and
refreshment stand. Skip the wooded trail unless you are
in the mood to stretch your legs. The castle is open daily
from Memorial Day through Columbus Day 11:00 a.m. to
5:00 p.m., and on weekends only Columbus Day through
mid-December from 10:00 a.m. to 4:00 p.m. The grounds
are open throughout the year.

▲**Connecticut River Museum**—On the waterfront at
the end of Main Street in Essex, the museum's exhibits
pertain to river history. The museum is open April
through December, Tuesday through Sunday from 10:00
a.m. to 5:00 p.m. Admission is $3 for adults, children
under 12 free.

▲▲**Steam Train and Riverboat Ride**—On Railroad
Avenue in Essex, this excursion offers a good alternative
way to see the Connecticut River and sights such as
Gillette's Castle and Goodspeed's Opera House if you're
tired of driving or if you fancy steam-powered locomo-
tives. All trains connect with a riverboat cruise, except
the last one of the day. Tickets cost $12.95 for adults,
$5.95 for children 2 to 11, children under 2 free, for the
combined train and riverboat trip, less for the train ride
only. The combined trip takes over two hours; separate
tickets are not sold for the riverboat cruise. The service

operates May through October. Call ahead for departure times as they vary from day to day and from season to season, (203) 767-0103.

Lodging

The **Tourist Information Center** at the Mystic exit will help you find lodging. There is a board listing nearby accommodations, their rates, and driving distances. The center's helpful personnel will even call ahead to secure your room. While there, be sure to peruse the menus from area restaurants and pick out the ones that best suit your tastes and budget. The tourist center is also a great source of area sightseeing information.

The **Inn at Mystic**, at the junction of Routes 27 and US 1, has accommodations ranging from motor court rooms to comfortable rooms in a traditional country inn. There are gardens, a tennis court, a restaurant, a pool, and a hot tub on the premises. Rooms in the motor court are $95 to $145 during the summer and $75 to $95 off-season. Rooms at the inn go for $165 to $195 per night. Call (800) 237-2415 or (203) 536-9604 for reservations.

If you wish to stay within walking distance of Mystic's downtown shops and restaurants, **The Whaler's Inn**, offering simple, motel-like accommodations and senior citizen discounts, is your only lodging choice in Mystic center. Doubles range from $65 to $125 per night. Call (203) 536-1506 or (800)243-2588.

Camping

Seaport Campground, 3 miles from Mystic Seaport Museum, is the closest campground to Mystic's attractions. From Exit 90 on Interstate 95, take Route 27 north for one and a quarter miles to Route 184. Follow that east for about one-half mile and watch for the campground on your left. RV hookups and tent sites are available, as well as complete recreational facilities, including swimming, on the premises. Open seasonally, mid-April through late October. Call (203) 536-4044 for reservations.

Dining

The Griswold Inn, Essex, serves sandwiches and burgers for lunch and traditional New England fare for dinner in a lively atmosphere. A fine collection of firearms and maritime prints grace the walls of the Griswold's several dining rooms. Lunch is about $8 per person, and dinner entrées run from $15 to $20. Servings are hearty. The inn also has 25 guest rooms. Reservations are recommended for overnight lodging or weekend dinners. Call (203) 767-1776.

In the Mystic area, you'll find a number of reasonably priced restaurants and fast-food establishments in and around Olde Mystick Village, just off I-95. In downtown Mystic, **Mulligan's**, on the west side of the drawbridge, has moderately priced meals ranging from sandwiches to lobster (203-536-2674). Locals recommend **The Draw Bridge Inne**, a half block from the drawbridge on Main Street, offering specialties for seafarers and landlubbers alike. Dinner entrées are $13 and up (203-536-9653).

For a simple but filling meal, try an overstuffed sandwich at **2 Sisters Deli** on Pearl Street just off Main. For breakfast, try **Bee Bee Dairy**, a family-style restaurant on Main Street, or **The Binnacle**, which has a very casual atmosphere and filling breakfasts.

Itinerary Option

Those who wish to extend their New England vacation southward to explore the exclusive Hamptons or sand dunes at Montauk can take the ferry from New London, Connecticut (several miles south of Mystic), to Orient Point on Long Island, New York. The ferry costs over $20 one-way for most automobiles including the driver, and you really do need to bring your car across to do any sightseeing. The ferry operates year-round except for Christmas Day. Sailing time is approximately one and a half hours. Call (203) 443-5281 for schedule and reservation information. From Orient Point, take Route 25 west to Riverhead where you pick up Route 24. Follow Route 24 until it intersects with Route 27. Drive east on Route 27 to the Hamptons, then continue all the way out to the lighthouse at Montauk Point.

MYSTIC

Early New Englanders were dependent on the ocean for
food, fuel (in the form of whale oil for lanterns), and
goods brought from abroad. The importance of the sea
comes to life in Mystic Seaport's re-creation of a nineteenth-century maritime village.

Travel Route: Mystic to Newport (45 miles)
From Mystic center, travel along coastal US 1 to Route 138
east. Cross over to Jamestown, then take the Jamestown
toll bridge to Newport. Several miles north of Mystic you
may want to take a short detour on Route 1A to see the
handsome village of Stonington.

Mystic to Newport

Sightseeing Highlights
▲▲▲**Mystic Seaport Museum**—The entrance to the
village is on Route 27 east less than one mile from I-95.
You'll need the better part of a day to explore the
museum grounds fully. Climb aboard a whaling vessel

to see the cramped quarters of deckhands and where whale blubber was processed; visit seaport shops typical of those that would have served a fishing community 100 years ago; watch boat builders at work; learn how fishermen navigated by the stars, in the planetarium; and see how sailing, once a necessary skill, has become a modern sport, in a special tribute to the America's Cup. General admission to the village, at $14.50 for adults, $8.75 for children 6 to 15, is rather expensive, but due to the vast number of exhibits the Seaport has to offer, the money is well spent. Separate tickets must be purchased if you wish to take one of the steamboat cruises that leave from the village or to visit the museum's planetarium. For a fast-food lunch of clam cakes, burgers, or hot dogs, there is a snack bar in the village; for more refined dining, try the Seaman's Inne next to the complex. The museum is open daily in the spring from 9:00 a.m. to 5:00 p.m., in summer from 9:00 a.m. to 8:00 p.m., in the fall and winter from 9:00 a.m. to 4:00 p.m., closed Christmas.

▲**Mystic Marinelife Aquarium**—Just off I-95 at the Mystic Exit, this is a worthwhile stop if you didn't make it to the New England Aquarium in Boston and have extra time after visiting the Seaport. Entrance fees are $8 for adults, $7 for seniors, $5 for children 5 to 12. The aquarium is open daily from 9:00 a.m. to 5:30 p.m. July 1 through Labor Day and 9:00 a.m. to 4:30 p.m. during the rest of the year. It is closed Thanksgiving, Christmas, New Year's Day, and the last week in January.

▲**Denison Pequotsepos Nature Center**—The 125-acre center, on Pequotsepos Road in Mystic, is comprised of self-guided nature trails and a small natural history museum. One trail is designed especially for blind visitors. The center is open May through October, Monday through Saturday 9:00 a.m. to 5:00 p.m., Sunday 11:00 to 5:00 p.m. During the winter months, it is open Tuesday through Saturday from 9:00 a.m. to 4:00 p.m. and Sunday 12:00 to 4:00 p.m. Admission is $1 for adults, 50 cents for children over 6.

Olde Mystic Village—It is probably best to pass on this group of souvenir shops and informal eating establishments adjacent to the aquarium unless you have plenty of time to kill.

Newport Lodging

Stay in the heart of things at the **Inntowne** on the corner of Thames and Mary streets where many of the shops and restaurants of Newport are at your doorstep. Rates range from $115 to $175 depending on the season and type of accommodation. Call (401) 846-9200 or (800) 457-7803 for reservations.

The **Marriott** on the waterfront is also convenient to Newport center. Nine of the Marriott's rooms are specially equipped for handicapped guests. Doubles run from about $145 to $220. Call Marriott's toll-free number, (800) 458-3066, or the hotel directly at (401) 849-1000.

If you like to be centrally located, there are two comfortable bed and breakfast establishments on quiet Clarke Street. The **Admiral Farragut** (401-846-4256 or 800-343-2863) at 31 Clarke was built in 1650. Their doubles range from $80 to $105 during the summer and start at $50 during the winter. Two of the nicest hosts in Newport, Sam and Rita Rogers, run the **Melville House** (401-847-0640) at 39 Clarke Street. The inn, built in 1750, is listed on the National Register of Historic Places. Doubles are $40 to $55 in the winter, and $75 to $100 in the summer including breakfast. For an out-of-the ordinary night's sleep, try the **Jailhouse Inn** (401-847-4638) where bars on the windows and black-and-white striped bedspreads are not just for show—the inn was once a jail. It is at 13 Marlborough Street, just around the corner from the Brick Marketplace, and doubles with continental breakfast range from $80 to $145. At the **Willows of Newport**, about a five minute walk from the Brick Marketplace, guests are served breakfast in bed by attendants in black-tie on bone china and a silver tea service. Hostess Pattie Murphy, a long-time resident of Newport, is happy to share her knowledge of Newport's diverse history with her guests. Doubles range from $88 to $135.

For a splurge you won't soon forget, stay at the **Inn at Castle Hill** off Ocean Drive. With a room overlooking the ocean, you'll feel almost like a Vanderbilt. Doubles with a private bath and water view are $180 during the summer, significantly less during the winter months. The inn's restaurant is also well worth a try (401-849-3800).

Bed & Breakfast of Rhode Island (401-849-1298) can also help you locate accommodations. Their service is free of charge.

Camping
There are several municipal campgrounds near Newport, the closest being **Middletown Campground** on Second Beach in neighboring Middletown. Since there are only 44 campsites, reservations are strongly recommended. Call (401) 846-5781. Open May through early October. Facilities include toilets, showers, and sewer hookups.

On the far side of the island, **Melville Ponds Campground** off Route 114 in Portsmouth has tent sites, RV sites with hookups, and recreational facilities. Open April 1 through October 31. Call (401) 849-8212.

If all campgrounds on the island are filled, try the campground in Jamestown at **Fort Getty Recreation Area**. You can fish at the campground, but you will have to cross the toll bridge to sightsee in Newport. Open during the summer months on a first come, first served basis. Tent sites are $17 per night, and RV hookups are $22 per night. Call (401) 423-7211 for directions and additional information.

Newport Dining
The **Black Pearl** (401-846-5264) on Bannister's Wharf is a very popular Newport restaurant, as evidenced by the throngs of hungry diners in line to be seated. Because of its reputation, the restaurant can be crowded and the service slow. Next door at the **Clarke Cooke House** (401-849-2900), you'll find truly elegant dining upstairs for dinner and a more casual atmosphere downstairs at the **Candy Store**. For dining in unique settings, try the **La Forge Restaurant** overlooking the grass courts at the Newport Casino, serving veal and chicken dinner entrées that run about $10; **The Moorings** situated in the famous New York Yacht Club on Sayer's Wharf (401-846-2260); or the **White Horse Tavern**, the oldest operating tavern in the United States (401-849-3600). Numerous restaurants along Thames Street offer cheaper alternatives for eating out.

For dessert, visit any one of the **Newport Creamery**'s several locations for a traditional ice cream cone. **Poor Richard's** at 254 Thames Street is the place to get breakfast, from pancakes to omelets.

Itinerary Option

Need a break from vigorous sightseeing? Need a break from the world in general? Then a trip to Block Island may just be the antidote. Only 12 miles off the coast of Rhode Island, Block Island was originally settled in 1661. The island offers visitors all of the quiet beauty, miles of beach, and dramatic cliffs of Martha's Vineyard, without the commercialism.

If you enjoy cycling past sand dunes, beach roses, lily ponds, and old stone walls, exploring wildlife refuges and lighthouses, or just lounging on the beach, Block Island will be a welcome retreat. But if you're looking for art museums, chic shops, and active nightlife, then this is not the place for you. There is only one town on the island, consisting primarily of one main street lined with Victorian era hotels and a handful of restaurants and souvenir shops.

Ferries to the island operate from Point Judith, Rhode Island, year-round, though a winter visit is not recommended. (To get to the ferry, travel north on US 1 from Mystic, and follow signs to Point Judith and the ferry.) Service is more frequent during the summer, and ferries even run from Newport during the summer months. The trip from Point Judith takes a little over an hour. One-way fares are $6.60 for adults, $3.15 for children, and $10.50 and $5, respectively, for a same-day round-trip. Passenger cars cost $20.25 one way, motorcycles are $11.85, and bicycles are $1.75. Call (401) 783-4613 for reservations and a current ferry schedule. If you're lucky enough to get a legal parking spot along the street, parking is free. Otherwise it will cost you about $5 per day.

Once on the island, just about every service you'll need is within a block of the ferry dock. The tourist booth in the dock parking lot can provide you with a map of the island for $1. It will guide you to the unusual gray granite lighthouse at Sandy Point, Crescent Beach, the Clayhead

Nature Trail, or the wildlife refuge at Rodman's Hollow. The map, and your sense of direction, is about all you'll need to find your way around this small island.

Across the street from the dock area you can rent a bike or moped, then shop for picnic foods at the Seaside Market next door (about the only place on the island to get provisions). While bringing your car over to the island may be cheaper than renting bikes for a family (about $10 per day per bicycle) or mopeds (about $60 per day for two), these two-wheeled vehicles bring you closer to the island's down-to-earth charm.

Most of the island's accommodations are right along Old Harbor's main street. (Some have limited seasons, so be sure to call ahead if you plan to stay overnight.) The **National Hotel**, built in 1888, is the most prominent. You can't miss it as the ferry pulls into the harbor. Doubles are $75 to $210 depending on the season and type of view. Call (401) 466-2901 or 800-225-2449 for reservations. The **Surf Hotel** (401-466-2241) and the **Inn at Old Harbor** (401-466-2212) with doubles including continental breakfast ranging from $85 to $140 are two other Victorian inns right in the town's center. The **Hotel Manisses** and the **1661 Inn**, both on the edge of town, are jointly managed. Guests staying at either can enjoy a small animal farm behind the Manisses Hotel, buffet breakfasts, and dinner at the hotel. The hotel has one of the most interesting menus on the island; dinner entrées are priced from $14.50 to $26.50. Room rates range from $80 to $300 (401-466-2421).

After visiting the island, you can pick up the 2 to 22 Days itinerary again by following US 1 north from Point Judith to Route 138. Take Route 138 east to Newport.

NEWPORT

Newport, on Aquidneck Island, is a city of contrasts: from the wealthy, some of whom still inhabit turn-of-the-century mansions, to military personnel stationed at the naval base, to the yachting crowd that routinely invades Newport each summer. Somehow this city manages to satisfy all of these groups in their varied pursuits. Today you'll discover why.

Suggested Schedule

9:00 a.m.	Breakfast.
10:00 a.m.	Tour one of Newport's sumptuous mansions.
11:30 a.m.	Take Ocean Drive and stop for a picnic lunch at Brenton Point State Park.
1:00 p.m.	Visit another luxurious "cottage."
2:30 p.m.	Promenade along the Cliff Walk, skirting the great lawns of many of Newport's finest homes and the ocean some thirty feet below.
3:30 p.m.	See the Tennis Hall of Fame or the Touro Synagogue, or spend the rest of the afternoon browsing at the Brick Marketplace, Bannister's Wharf, or along Thames Street.
6:00 p.m.	Dinner.
8:00 p.m.	Relax to the beat of a local band in one of Newport's many bars, or watch a jai alai match.

Travel Route
All of today's driving will be within Newport itself. Ocean Drive can be reached either from the downtown waterfront area by following the signs to Ocean Drive or by traveling past the mansions on Bellevue Avenue and taking a left when you get to the end of Bellevue.

Newport "Cottages"

The Preservation Society of Newport operates six exquisite mansions, or "cottages" as they were called by their
original owners, one historic home, and a topiary garden.
You will probably have time to visit only two properties
in one day unless you're very energetic. Take your pick.

Marble House and Château-Sur-Mer are open throughout the winter from 10:00 a.m. to 4:00 p.m. on weekends
and are beautifully decorated for Christmas. Most of the
remaining mansions are open weekends starting in April,
and all are open daily throughout the summer from 10:00
a.m. to 5:00 p.m. The Breakers is open from 9:30 a.m. to
6:00 p.m. July through Labor Day. Since the hours do vary
from mansion to mansion, and from season to season, it is
best to check with the Preservation Society (401-847-1000)
for hours during your visit. Admission to most of the mansions is $7 for adults, $4 for children 6 to 11. Reduced
rates are available when you purchase combination tickets
to more than one mansion. The combination tickets range

from $11 for any two mansions to $32.50 if you wish to visit them all.

The Breakers, on Ochre Point Avenue off Bellevue, is the most extravagant of all the mansions and the most popular with tourists. Built in an Italian Renaissance style for Cornelius Vanderbilt in 1895, this stately home with an abundance of gold leaf and marble throughout its interior is almost overwhelmingly opulent. Children will enjoy the "Children's Cottage" on the grounds.

Château-Sur-Mer ("House by the Sea") and **Rosecliff** (on Bellevue Avenue) are situated on the ocean as well. Château-Sur-Mer has a Chinese Moon Gate on its grounds. Rosecliff was designed by well-known architect Stanford White and has the largest private ballroom in Newport. Robert Redford and Mia Farrow waltzed in this ballroom in the movie version of *The Great Gatsby.*

Marble House on Bellevue Avenue is my personal favorite. Appropriately named for the beautiful and rare marble throughout, the "cottage" was built for William K. Vanderbilt in 1892. A Chinese teahouse on the grounds exemplifies fascination of the moneyed class with the Orient at the turn of the century.

Also on Bellevue Avenue are **The Elms** and **Kingscote**. The Elms, modeled after a French château, is known for its array of trees and shrubbery. Kingscote, built in 1839, is one of the oldest mansions open to the public. Incorporating elements of both Victorian and Gothic architecture, the estate was named after William Henry King, who acquired the property in 1864.

The **Hunter House** at 54 Washington Street is much smaller in scale than the grand "cottages," reflecting its mid-eighteenth-century time period. It was the headquarters for French naval forces during the Revolutionary War and is a National Historic Landmark.

The Green Animals topiary gardens are located on Cory's Lane off Route 114 north in Portsmouth. An elephant, a giraffe, and a camel are just a few of the animal-shaped shrubs that are bound to amuse children and adults alike.

Several other stately homes, not operated by the Preservation Society, are also open to the public. **Hammersmith Farms**, near Fort Adams, is often considered the most "livable" of the Newport mansions. The wedding reception for John F. and Jackie Kennedy was held here. Its colorful gardens were designed by Frederick Law Olmstead. Open weekends in March and November, daily April through October from 10:00 a.m. to 5:00 p.m. At the height of the summer season, hours are extended to 7:00 p.m.

Bellecourt Castle on Bellevue Avenue is still owned and occupied by the Tinney family. The house is open for high tea and guided tours by attendants in period costume. A gold coronation coach and art treasures from all over the world are among the items on display. Admission is $6 for adults, $5 for seniors, $3.50 for students, $2 for children 6 to 12, and $10 for a family of two adults and their children. The house is open daily from 9:00 a.m. to 5:00 p.m. during the summer and is closed January through mid-February. Call (401) 846-0669 for museum hours if you plan to visit during the spring or fall.

Beechwood, also on Bellevue Avenue, was built for the Astors. Although the home is not as lavish or well kept as the Preservation Society mansions, the tour can be quite entertaining: actors playing members of the Astor household greet you as a dinner guest and treat you to family gossip of the day. A "calling card" is $7 for adults, $5.50 for children and senior citizens, and $30 for a family. The house is open from 10:00 a.m. to 4:00 p.m. on weekends February through mid-May, from 10:00 a.m. to 5:00 p.m. daily mid-May through October, and daily from 10:00 to 4:00 p.m. November through mid-December. It is closed from mid-December through January.

The grand mansions of Newport are not the only homes that merit a look while you're here. There are many beautifully restored colonial homes in and around Queen Anne Square one block from Thames Street. Explore these streets on your own or take an organized walking tour with the Newport Historical Society. The Society is located at 82 Touro Street, and tours usually begin at 10:00 a.m. in the summer. Call (401) 846-0813 for additional exact schedules and cost.

Other Sightseeing Highlights
▲**Touro Synagogue**—Built in 1763, the oldest synagogue in the country is now a National Historic Site. Summer hours are 10:00 a.m. to 5:00 p.m. daily, except Saturday. Winter visitors call (401) 847-4794 for an appointment.

▲**Tennis Hall of Fame**—The museum is adjacent to the emerald green grass courts of the Newport Casino. The casino was built in 1880, and professional tennis tournaments are still held there today. Tennis buffs will no doubt want to visit the museum, but those who don't play will probably be content to poke around the outside of the building. Admission to the museum is $5 for adults, $2.50 for youths under 16. Senior citizen discounts are available. The museum is open from 10:00 a.m. to 5:00 p.m. June through September and 11:00 a.m. to 4:00 p.m. the rest of the year.

Should you wish to view the island from a two-wheeled vehicle, you can rent bicycles from **Ten Speed Spokes** at the corner of Elm and America's Cup Avenue (401-847-5609).

Shopping
The Brick Marketplace on Thames Street and Bannisters and Bowen wharves off America's Cup Avenue comprise Newport's main shopping district. Not to be missed by nautical buffs is the **Armchair Sailor Bookstore** on Lee's Wharf, which has one of the most comprehensive selections anywhere of maritime publications.

Nightlife
Jai alai is considered to be the fastest game on two feet, and you may wish to view a match or two at **Newport Jai Alai**, 150 Admiral Kalbfus Road. Rhode Island is one of the few states that allows parimutuel wagering on the sport. Admission is nominal to encourage betting, which some find similar to playing the horses. Call 800-451-2500 or (401) 849-5000 for schedule and information.

Many of Newport's bars and restaurants offer musical entertainment in the evenings. Try **The Ark** on Thames Street for jazz. **Cobblestones**, also on Thames, has live entertainment on weekends and a piano bar. **Club Thames** on America's Cup Avenue is the place to go for dancing to a contemporary beat.

NEW BEDFORD AND SANDWICH

Leaving Newport's tycoons behind, you will learn about
more customary nineteenth-century New England occupa-
tions such as whaling in New Bedford and glass-making
in Sandwich.

Suggested Schedule	
9:00 a.m.	Leave Newport for New Bedford.
10:00 a.m.	Visit Whaling Museum.
11:00 a.m.	Stroll through New Bedford's renovated historic district and sit down to an early lunch.
12:30 p.m.	Travel to Cape Cod.
1:30 p.m.	Sandwich Glass Museum.
2:30 p.m.	Heritage Plantation.
5:00 p.m.	Check into lodging.
6:00 p.m.	Early dinner and quiet evening to prepare for an early departure in the morning.

Travel Route: Newport to Sandwich (62 miles)
From Newport, take Route 114 north to Route 24 north
toward Tiverton and Fall River. At Fall River get on
Interstate 195 east toward Cape Cod. Take Exit 15 to
Route 18 for New Bedford's historic quarter and follow
signs to the visitor center.

After stopping in New Bedford, return to I-195 east.
Take Exit 22A for Route 25 to Cape Cod and the Islands
via the Bourne Bridge. There is a rotary at the end of the
bridge. Follow the rotary three-quarters of the way around
to US 6 east toward Sagamore. As you approach the
Sagamore Bridge, go straight onto Route 6A east for
Sagamore and Sandwich. When you get to Sandwich,
there will be a sign to the center, which is about one-half
mile from Route 6A to your right.

New Bedford Sightseeing Highlights
Once a bustling whaling center, New Bedford experienced a great decline during the twentieth century.

Newport to Sandwich

Recently, efforts have been made to restore the city to its
past glory. You can see the handsome result of those
efforts by rambling through the 16-block cobblestone area
that comprises the historic district, originally built up in
the 1760s. In its heyday, 10,000 people from New Bedford
made their living in the whaling trade. New Bedford's visitor center is on Second Street in the historic district. It is
open Monday through Saturday 9:00 a.m. to 5:00 p.m.,
Sunday 11:00 a.m. to 5:00 p.m.

▲▲**Whaling Museum**—Exhibits here, ranging from
model vessels and ship's logs to artwork depicting whaling expeditions, will give you a fascinating look at an
industry and an era that have long since died out. Open
Monday through Saturday 9:00 a.m. to 5:00 p.m., Sunday
from 1:00 to 5:00 p.m. During the summer, Sunday hours
are 11:00 a.m. to 5:00 p.m. Admission is $3.50 for adults,
$3 for seniors, $2.50 for children 6 to 14. After visiting the
museum, you may want to visit the **Seaman's Bethel**
across the street: it was the whalemen's chapel referred
to in Herman Melville's *Moby Dick*.

▲**Rotch-Jones-Duff House & Garden Museum**—Built in
what is now New Bedford's County Street Historic District,

this 1834 Greek Revival home is a fine example of the "brave houses and flowery gardens" Melville described in *Moby Dick*. The museum is open during the summer from 11:00 a.m. to 4:00 p.m. Tuesday through Saturday. Admission is $3 for adults, $1.50 for seniors, and $1 for children over 12. On some summer evenings, the museum offers concerts under the stars. Call (508) 977-1401 for more information.

Sandwich Sightseeing Highlights
The town of Sandwich celebrated its 350th birthday in 1987. It is the quintessential Cape Cod town, with well-kept shingled houses, gentle tidal marshes, and many sights to occupy the out-of-town visitor.

▲▲**Heritage Plantation**—The plantation is on Grove and Pine streets. To get there, turn left onto Grove Street next to the town hall in Sandwich center. The parking lot will be on your left approximately one-half mile from the center. The prettiest time to visit the plantation is in early June when the rhododendrons are in full bloom, but the beautifully landscaped 76-acre grounds are handsome in any season. American folk art, Currier & Ives lithographs, antique firearms, and early automobiles are among the plantation's other attractions. The antique cars, housed in a replica of the Shaker Round Barn at Hancock, include a vibrant green and yellow Duesenberg designed for Gary Cooper which will delight auto buffs. The art museum houses a carousel to entertain the children while you view the Currier & Ives collection. Buses run at regular intervals between the museums. Admission is $7 for adults, $6 for seniors, $3 for children 6 to 12, and there is no charge for children 5 and under. The plantation is open May through October from 10:00 a.m. to 5:00 p.m. daily, although tickets are not sold after 4:15 p.m. Picnicking on the grounds is not allowed.

▲**Sandwich Glass Museum**—Across from Town Hall Square in Sandwich center, the museum houses a fine collection of glassware made in the 1800s by the Boston & Sandwich Glass Company and the Cape Cod Glass Works. Exhibits include an explanation of glass manufacturing procedures and a chronology of the Sandwich operation. Open daily from 9:30 a.m. to 4:30 p.m. April through October, closed during January, and open the remaining months Wednesday through Sunday from 9:30 a.m. to 4:00 p.m. Admission is $3 for adults, 50 cents for children over 5.

In Sandwich, you can also visit a number of historic homes, all within a three-block radius of Town Hall Square. There's a water-operated stone mill, **Dexter's Grist Mill**, and **Hoxie House**, the oldest house on Cape Cod, originally built in the 1600s and restored in 1960. Admission to the mill is $1.50 for adults, 75 cents for children 12 to 16. Hoxie House is open Monday through Saturday from 10:00 a.m. to 5:00 p.m. (last tour 4:15 p.m.), and Sundays from 1:00 p.m. to 5:00 p.m. June through October. Admission is $1.50 for adults, 75 cents for children. Combination tickets to both sites are $2.50 for adults, $1 for children.

Yesteryears Doll Museum, in the First Parish Meetinghouse, has a collection of rare and antique dolls and dollhouses. It is open Monday through Saturday from 10:00 a.m. to 4:00 p.m. May through October. Admission is $3 for adults, $2.50 for seniors, and $2 for children.

The **Thornton Burgess Museum**, just up the street from the mill, was the home of the children's books author, and some of his works and original artwork is on display here. If you're traveling with small fans of Peter Rabbit and the famous briar patch, then you may want to visit the **Green Briar Nature Center and Jam Kitchen** on Discovery Hill Road off Route 6A east of Sandwich between Sandwich center and Quaker Meeting House Road. You can watch homemade jams bubbling away in the kitchen, visit "Peter Rabbit," then take the nature trail around the "old briar patch" that served as an inspiration for Burgess's marvelous children's tales. Both the museum and the jam kitchen are open Monday through Saturday 10:00 a.m. to 4:00 p.m., Sunday from 1:00 p.m. to 4:00 p.m. During July and August, there is storytelling at the museum.

If you're a potato chip lover, you may want to tour the **Cape Cod Chip Factory** in Hyannis on Breeds Hill Road in Independence Park off route 132 opposite the Cape Cod Mall. The tour is self-guided, free, and you even get a complimentary bag of chips at the end of the tour. The factory is open for tours Monday through Friday from 10:00 a.m. to 4:00 p.m.

Lodging

On Sandwich's Main Street, the **Dan'l Webster Inn** (508-888-3622 or 800-444-3566) will bathe you in four-star comfort you won't have to sell your soul for. The dining room has a fine reputation, serving such favorites as chateaubriand ($24.95) and baked scrod in lobster sauce ($15.95). Double rooms run from $89 to $165 per night depending on the season. Reservations are strongly recommended.

Sandwich also has a handful of choice bed and breakfasts, all in the town center. Across the street from the Dan'l Webster, friendly hosts greet you at the **Captain Ezra Nye Guesthouse** (800-388-2278 or 508-888-6142) built in 1829. Rates, $55 to $85 per night including breakfast, are quite reasonable for the area. The **Isaiah Jones Homestead** (508-888-9115 or 800-526-1625), also on Main Street, is elegantly furnished with four-poster beds and other Victorian pieces. Modern conveniences are not overlooked, as one room has its own jacuzzi tub. Doubles range from $65 to $119. Lovely handmade quilts adorn the beds at The **Summer House** at 158 Main Street. The inn has a pleasant sun porch, and afternoon tea and a full breakfast are included in the nightly rate of $50 to $75. Call (508) 888-4991.

You'll find a wide assortment of motor inns and cottages along scenic 6A in Sandwich. On the upper end is the mock Tudor-style **Earl of Sandwich Motor Manor** (508-888-1415 or 800-442-EARL), with doubles ranging from $50 to $85. The small cedar-shingled **Spring Garden Motel** (508-888-0710) with flowering window boxes is in East Sandwich on the edge of a tidal marsh. Continental breakfast is included in the room rate, and rooms start at $55 in high season. If you would like to wake up to a rooster crowing and other sounds of a working farm,

Wingscorton Farm Inn (508-888-0534), across the road from the Spring Garden Motel, offers fine accommodations ($115 to $150 per night including a full breakfast).

For those traveling on a budget, the **HyLand Youth Hostel** at 465 Falmouth Road in nearby Hyannis is not too far from the ferryboat docks. The hostel is open all year and also offers facilities for families and couples. Beds are $10 per person. Call (508) 775-2970 for information.

Camping

Shawme Crowell State Forest on Route 130 in Sandwich has 280 sites and is open April through November (508-888-0351). **Peter's Pond Park** in Sandwich has both tent and trailer sites. Located on a freshwater pond, the campground is open seasonally mid-April through mid-October. Sites start at $17 per night (508-477-1775).

Dining

In New Bedford for lunch, **Freestone's Restaurant & Bar** is located in an attractive building on the corner of Williams and Second streets. It serves seafood-melt sandwiches and the like at reasonable prices; entrées are more expensive (around $12 apiece). **Jimmy Connor's Irish Pub**, on the corner of Acushnet and Union streets, is a good place to stop for a casual burger and draft beer at a modest price. **The Last Laugh** is a bar and deli just north of the historic district where you can sample sandwiches named for famous comedians such as Jackie Gleason.

For dinner, if the Dan'l Webster is too steep for your budget, try **Sandy's** (508-888-6480), a family-style restaurant just north of Sandwich on 6A. The fried clams are marvelous, but bring a hearty appetite as the portions are huge. Just a little farther north on 6A is the **Sagamore Inn** (508-888-9707), a favorite with locals. The atmosphere is very lively, and the fare includes fresh seafood, New England-style dinners, and Italian specialties. **Michael's at Sandy Neck**, on Route 6A in East Sandwich, specializes in seafood. Prices are moderate. **O'Brien's**, just next door, is the place to go for homemade ice cream. (There's also an O'Brien's on 6A adjacent to the turnoff for Sandwich

Center.) If your lodging does not provide breakfast, try the
casual Marshland Restaurant on 6A near Sandwich center.
Portions are large, but the prices aren't.

Nightlife
The **Cape Cod Melody Tent** in Hyannis features well-
known singers, comedians, and rock groups throughout
the summer. Call (508) 775-9100 for schedule and ticket
information.

Itinerary Options
Bargain hunters with time to spare may profit from
prospecting the New Bedford/Fall River area factory outlet
stores. These stores are factory outlets in the truest sense
since they are generally located on the premises of the
factory. A guide to the outlets can be picked up at the
New Bedford visitor center.

The world's largest exhibit of historic fighting ships can
be found in Fall River's **Battleship Cove**. Visitors can tour
the USS *Joseph P. Kennedy Jr.* destroyer, a 35,000-ton
battleship called "Big Mamie" that saw action in WWII,
a WWII attack sub, and PT boats. Call (508) 678-1100 for
information. The **Marine Museum** at Fall River nearby
has ship models, a Titanic exhibit, and other marine
collections. The museum is open 9:00 a.m. to 5:00 p.m.
Monday through Friday, 10:00 a.m. to 5:00 p.m. on weekends and holidays. Admission is $3 for adults, $1 for
children under 14.

MARTHA'S VINEYARD

Although much of your New England trip so far has been
spent along the coastline where day-to-day life was, and
in some areas still is, tied to the ocean, you'll spend the
next two days visiting islands whose main lifeline to
"civilization" is the sea. The itinerary is planned so that
you can spend one day on Martha's Vineyard and one
day on Nantucket. The islands are meant to be toured at
a relaxed pace, however, so you may want to travel to
just one of them and spread the sightseeing highlights out
over two days—or allow more time on each island if you
can. The inter–island ferry only runs from early July
through mid-September, so if you are traveling during any
other month, you will probably have to limit yourself to
just one island.

Suggested Schedule

8:15 a.m.	Leave Sandwich for the Hyannis docks.
9:15 a.m.	Ferry leaves for Martha's Vineyard.
11:00 a.m.	Arrive in Oak Bluffs, then travel to Gay Head.
12:30 p.m.	Have lunch and see the jagged cliffs at Gay Head.
1:30 p.m.	Leave Gay Head for Edgartown.
2:30 p.m.	Take your choice: stroll past stately mansions from the whaling era, or shop for souvenirs in lovely Edgartown, or soak up the sun on a quiet beach on Chappaquiddick or along Beach Road between Edgartown and Oak Bluffs.
6:00 p.m.	Check into accommodations.
7:00 p.m.	Dinner.

Travel Route: Sandwich to Ferry Docks in Hyannis (10 miles)

From Sandwich center, travel to Hyannis by Route 6A east
until it intersects with Route 132. Turn right on Route 132.

When you reach Hyannis, there will be a rotary and signs to the ferry docks. (If you plan to travel to Nantucket or Martha's Vineyard for the day only, there is free parking on South Street about two blocks from the docks. The parking lots are marked by a blue shell sign with a large "P" in the center of the shell. Cars may not be left over-night in the free parking lots.) Long-term parking at the docks costs about $6 per day. Should you wish to take your car to Martha's Vineyard, you'll need to take the ferry from Woods Hole, which is described below as a route option.

Steamship Authority boats leave from South Street and travel to and from Nantucket only; Hy-Line Boats to both Nantucket and Martha's Vineyard leave from Ocean Street, which intersects with South Street. Because of their proximity to one another, and because fares from Nantucket (around $10.75 for adults and $5.25 for children 5 and over) are roughly the same on both lines, it is possible to take the Hy-Line out to the islands and return by the Steamship Authority, or vice versa, giving you more departure times to choose from. Sailing time from Hyannis to Oak Bluffs is approximately one hour and 45 minutes, and roughly two hours to Nantucket (some of the Hy-Line boats can do it in an hour and 45 minutes).

You will arrive on Martha's Vineyard in Oak Bluffs. Rent a moped and ride southwest toward West Tisbury. From West Tisbury, travel along Middle Road to Chilmark, and from Chilmark follow signs to Gay Head. If you're picnicking, turn right about five miles outside of Chilmark at the sign for Lobsterville Beach. After lunch, return to the main road and continue to Gay Head to view the cliffs and lighthouse. If you didn't bring a picnic lunch, there are several fast-food establishments at Gay Head where you can get fried clam platters and the like.

From Gay Head, return to West Tisbury, then follow the Edgartown-West Tisbury road to Edgartown. Total distance from Gay Head to Edgartown is 21 miles.

Route Option: Visiting Martha's Vineyard one day and Nantucket the next, which involves a lot of travel time on ferries and the added expense of renting alternative

Martha's Vineyard

modes of transportation on the islands, may not allow
enough time for exploration of each island. Should you
decide to visit only Martha's Vineyard, take the ferry from
Woods Hole instead of Hyannis. It is faster and cheaper.
To get to Woods Hole from Sandwich, take Route 6A west
to Sagamore, then follow US 6 west to Bourne. From
Bourne, take Route 28 east to Falmouth and follow signs
to the docks. The first ferry to the Vineyard usually leaves
around 7:00 a.m. in the summer, and sailing time is
approximately 45 minutes. Boats leaving from Woods
Hole arrive in either Oak Bluffs or Vineyard Haven,
only a few miles apart.

Passenger fares one-way from Woods Hole to Martha's
Vineyard are around $4.50 for adults, $2.25 for children
5 to 12. Automobiles are $36 one-way from mid-May
through mid-October and somewhat less expensive during the winter months. Reservations for automobiles are
strongly recommended during the summer months.
Although it may seem expensive to bring a car over, when
you consider that moped rentals are at least $50 a day, it
may be worth the fare, particularly if you decide to stay
more than one day or if there are more than two people
in your party. Call the Steamship Authority in Woods Hole

(508-540-2022) for the ferry schedule and reservation information.

Should you wish to spend all your time on Nantucket instead, call either Hy-line Cruises (508-778-2600) or the Steamship Authority (508-540-2022) in Hyannis for complete ferry information. Cars can travel on Steamship Authority ferries only, at a rate of $83 each way. Since Nantucket is such a small island, it really makes more sense to leave your car on the mainland and travel by other means once on the island.

Transportation on Martha's Vineyard
Mopeds are one of the easiest ways to get around the island. You don't have to worry about finding a parking space when you discover that deserted stretch of beach, and you can travel much faster than on a bicycle. The suggested schedule is designed for those traveling by moped; if you decide to bicycle instead, adjust your travel time accordingly. There are clearly marked and well-maintained bicycle paths on the island.

Moped and bicycle rental places abound in Vineyard Haven, Edgartown, and particularly Oak Bluffs. Many operations claim they have the lowest rates on the island. You may want to shop around, but my experience has been that rates tend to be fairly consistent from one place to the next and that your time is better spent sightseeing than looking for a bargain-priced moped rental. Daily rentals cost at least $50 in season for a moped that seats two fairly comfortably. Bicycle rentals run about $15 per day.

Numerous taxi services and sightseeing operators will greet you right at the boat and take you around the island, if you don't want to get around on your own steam.

Martha's Vineyard
Though Martha's Vineyard is only 7 miles from Cape Cod and the mainland, once you get there it doesn't take long to relax and leave the rest of the world behind. The island is 20 miles long by 10 miles wide at its widest point, and the population swells from around 12,000 year-round

residents to almost 62,000 during the summer. Even so, if you venture out of the main towns, you can almost always find a quiet spot to call your own.

Martha's Vineyard was named for an early settler's daughter and for the abundance of grapes that used to cover the island. Now the island is comprised of three main towns, Vineyard Haven, Oak Bluffs, and Edgartown, with stretches of white sand beach and sand dunes in between. Edgartown, the most elegant of the three, is another example of what great prosperity the whaling trade brought to nineteenth-century New England communities. Vineyard Haven is the quietest of the three, while Oak Bluffs, with its colorful Victorian "gingerbread" houses and active nightlife, is the most flamboyant.

Most people don't come to Martha's Vineyard to spend their time in museums, but if inclement weather forces you indoors, there is the **Old Schoolhouse Museum** on Main Street in Vineyard Haven run by the Historical Preservation Society. The museum is open Monday through Friday 10:00 a.m. to 2:00 p.m. from mid-June through mid-September. Admission is by donation. Also in Vineyard Haven, the **Jirah Luce House** displays nautical and other artifacts representing nineteenth-century island life, including a collection of Victorian dolls. It is on Beach Street and is open Tuesday through Saturday 10:00 a.m. to 4:30 p.m. from mid-June through mid-September. A small admission fee is charged.

In Edgartown on School Street, the **Dukes County Historical Society** operates a museum and library dedicated to preserving island history through its exhibits of maritime artifacts, scrimshaw, and antique clothing. It is open 10:00 a.m to 4:30 p.m. Tuesday through Saturday from mid-June through mid-September. Admission is $2 for adults, 50 cents for children. During the rest of the year the museum is open Wednesday through Friday 1:00 p.m. to 4:00 p.m., Saturday 10:00 a.m. to 4:00 p.m., and admission is free. Other indoor island activities include shopping in Edgartown, or if you're traveling with kids, the **Flying Horses Carousel** at the bottom of Circuit Avenue in Oak Bluffs.

Back outdoors, you may enjoy an excursion to **Chappaquiddick Island**. A ferry runs from the waterfront in Edgartown to the island from 7:30 a.m. to midnight during the summer. Fares are nominal, and prices are even quoted for horses and cattle in case you brought yours along. The ferry runs as needed and must be one of the shortest ferry crossings you'll ever experience. Moped riders may not find the trip worthwhile since the main road turns to sand several miles inland, and mopeds are not meant to operate in sand.

The beaches on the Vineyard are lovely. Perhaps the most accessible beach to the public is the **Joseph Silvia State Beach**, which runs along the road between Edgartown and Oak Bluffs. Just park your vehicle on the side of the road, hop over the dunes, and stretch out. Warning: as tempting as it may be, overnight camping is not allowed.

Helpful Hints

Those who plan to travel about the island by bicycle or moped should only bring over one small bag that will fit easily on your back or in the vehicle's basket. If you need to carry more than a daypack, be prepared to take a taxi to and from your hotel once on the island.

Lodging

For sumptuous accommodations in Edgartown, the **Charlotte Inn** on South Summer Street fits the bill while providing country inn comfort in restored nineteenth-century homes that originally belonged to sea captains. Doubles start at $195 and suites at $395 during the high season (508-627-4751). The lovely **Victorian Inn** on South Water Street was once a whaling captain's home as well and is now listed in the National Register of Historic Places. Prices are $97 to $198 in high season, and start at $55 in the off-season. Breakfast is included (508-627-4784). The **Daggett House** at 59 North Water Street (508-627-4600) was built in 1660, has a secret stairway, and is the only B&B on the water in Edgartown. Doubles are $70 to $175 including breakfast. The **Governor Bradford**

Inn, at 128 Main Street (508-627-9510), is also a hand-some home originally built for a sea captain. Doubles range from $60 to $195 including breakfast.

The **Oak Bluffs Inn**, at the corner of Circuit Avenue and Pequot Avenue in Oak Bluffs, is painted flamboyantly in pink to exemplify the lighter side of Victorian architecture. Rates range from $90 to $130 during the summer, and from $50 to $80 in the off season. Call (508) 693-7171 for reservations. The **Wesley Hotel** on Lake Avenue overlooking Oak Bluffs Harbor has been restored and is typical of many turn-of-the-century seaside hotels. In high season, double rooms with shared baths are $60, doubles with private baths are $110, and suites are $140 (505-693-6611 or 800-638-9027).

Perhaps the least expensive lodging on the island can be found at the **Manter Memorial AYH Hostel** on the Edgartown-West Tisbury Road three miles west of the airport. Dormitory-style accommodations cost about $10 per night per person. The hostel is open from April through November; call (508) 693-2665 for further information.

Camping

There are two campgrounds on Martha's Vineyard: **Webb's Camping Area** on Barnes Road several miles southwest of Oak Bluffs (508-693-0233) and **Martha's Vineyard Family Campground** on the Edgartown-Vineyard Haven road a little over a mile from the ferry dock (508-693-3772). Martha's Vineyard Family Campground is open from mid-May through mid-October, and nightly rates start at $20. Webb's Camping Area is open from mid-May through mid-September with nightly rates starting at $22. Both campgrounds have facilities for both RV and tent campers.

Dining

During the summer, the visitor has plenty of dining choices on the island. In Edgartown, the **Navigator Restaurant and Boathouse Bar** (508-627-4320) at the foot of Main Street and the **Wharf Restaurant** (508-627-9967) across the street both serve seafood. The Navigator overlooks the water, and lunches go for about $7.95, while dinner entrées run around $18.95. If your appetite runs to dishes such as roast rack of lamb Dijon, veal scaloppine, and prime rib, try the **Shiretown Inn & Restaurant** (508-627-3353). Dinner entrées start around $20, and there is a pub on the premises. **Andrea's Restaurant** (508-627-5850) on Upper Main Street features northern Italian cuisine in an elegant but comfortable setting. For the cheapest oceanfront table in town, get a burger or fried clams to go from **The Quarterdeck** stand near the Chappaquiddick ferry, and sit on the docks.

In Oak Bluffs, meals are usually casual, and on Circuit Avenue, you can get anything from steak and seafood at **David's Island House** to subs, pasta, and pizza at **Papa's Pizza** to fresh fish at the **Oyster Bar**.

Nightlife
Of the three main towns, Oak Bluffs has the most active nightlife on the Vineyard. The **Atlantic Connection Nightclub** as well as some of the neighboring bars on Circuit Avenue can be jam-packed during the summer months. Many of the patrons are college students working on the island during school break.

NANTUCKET

Thirty miles from the Massachusetts coast, Nantucket Island is a sparkling oasis in the Atlantic. Evidence of the island's onetime whaling prominence can be seen in the facades of graceful Federal, Greek Revival, and Georgian-style homes that border Nantucket town's cobblestone streets. Shingled cottages in Siasconset on the other side of the island are more modest, yet no less respectable, reminders of the seafaring life. In between are miles of low-lying moors and soft sand beaches.

Suggested Schedule

9:00 a.m.	Stroll around Oak Bluffs.
10:00 a.m.	Take ferry to Nantucket.
12:00 noon	Arrive in Nantucket and travel to Siasconset.
1:00 p.m.	Picnic on the beach in Siasconset.
3:00 p.m.	Return to the town of Nantucket and spend the rest of the afternoon exploring quaint narrow streets, attractive boutiques, and historic homes.
7:00 p.m.	Dinner.

Travel Route

Hy-Line (508-778-2600) operates an inter–island ferry from Oak Bluffs, Martha's Vineyard, to Nantucket from mid-June to September 15. The ferry takes passengers only. It departs Oak Bluffs three times a day and costs $10.75 for adults, $5.25 for children 5 and over. Bikes are $4.50.

Once on Nantucket, travel to Siasconset by following Main Street away from the docks to Orange Street. Turn left on Orange Street and follow it until you come to a rotary. At the rotary, take Milestone Road all the way to Siasconset. Affectionately known as "Sconset," Siasconset is 7½ miles from the town of Nantucket. For bicyclists, a paved bike path parallels the main road for most of the distance.

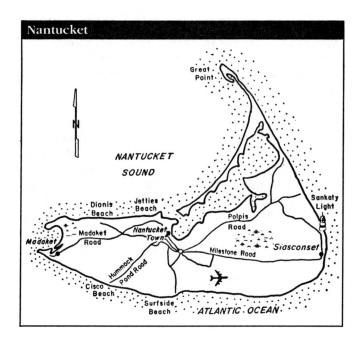

Sightseeing Highlights

In Siasconset, there are no official sights to see, but the town's often-deserted beach, quiet seaside lanes, and charming weathered cottages are enough to warrant the trip from Nantucket center. One of my favorite walks is along the footpath that runs between some of Sconset's most beautiful homes and the beach plum-covered sand dunes that serve as a protective barrier between the houses and the sea. To get to the footpath, go straight from the market in the town's center to the row of houses overlooking the beach. At the end of the row, at a house named "Casa Marina," turn right just to the left of the house on what looks like a driveway. Where the driveway veers back to the main road, continue straight ahead onto the lawn. This is the beginning of the footpath. The path will lead you across people's lawns—this is legal, but of course one must be considerate of their property. The path runs from the village out to Sankaty Head Lighthouse.

The **Nantucket Historical Association** (508-228-1894) operates a number of period homes, museums, and monuments, representing four centuries of Nantucket history. The sights are located throughout the town of Nantucket, so you should pick up the "Historic Nantucket" brochure, which maps out the route, from the tourist office on the corner of Chestnut Street, just one block from Main Street.

The tour begins at the **Thomas Macy Warehouse** on Straight Wharf, then continues to the **Whaling Museum** on Broad Street near Steamboat Wharf. Just next door is the **Peter Fougler Museum and Research Center** building where genealogical charts and ship's logs are on display. The period homes include **The Oldest House**, built in 1686 and considered to be the oldest house still standing on the island; **The Hawden House**, a stately Greek Revival built in 1845 at the height of the whaling era; and **The Macy-Christian House**. You can also visit the **Old Gaol**, or old jail, built in 1805; the **Old Mill**, built in 1746 and still operational today; the **Quaker Meeting House**, dating to 1838; the **Fair Street Museum** next door, containing Nantucket decorative arts exhibits; and the **Fire Hose Cart House**, which contains nineteenth-century firefighting equipment and was built in 1866.

Admission charges to the various buildings range from $3 to $4, or you can get a visitor's pass that will admit you to all of them for $8 for adults, $4 for children 5 to 14. You'll need at least three hours to take the entire tour. The buildings close at 5:00 p.m., so if you wish to visit them all, you will probably have to pass on the trip to Sconset or else travel to Sconset late in the day.

The **Maria Mitchell Science Center**, dedicated to the nation's first prominent woman astronomer, operates a science library, a small natural science museum, an aquarium, an observatory, and the astronomer's birthplace built in 1790. The center is open from 10:00 a.m. to 4:00 p.m. Tuesday through Saturday during the summer. Stop in at the library at 2 Vestal Street, or call (508) 228-9198 for details. The **Nantucket Life-Saving Museum** on Polpis Road outside of town claims to be the only museum of its kind in the world. It is open from mid-June through mid-

October from 10:00 a.m. to 4:00 p.m. Tuesday through Saturday. Admission is charged.

Those with extra time to beachcomb may also want to visit **Children's Beach, Jetties Beach**, and **South Beach**, all within walking distance from downtown Nantucket. **Dionis Beach**, three miles south of town, has still-water swimming, while more adventurous swimmers will enjoy the surf at **Madaket, Surfside**, and **Siasconset**. Serious surfers find **Cisco Beach** to their liking.

Nantucket is also a shopper's paradise with upscale antique stores, gift shops, boutiques, and galleries, as well as more touristy ice cream parlors, and T-shirt and souvenir shops. If you love to shop, plan to set aside some time for browsing in this haven.

Getting Around the Island
Nantucket is small and flat enough so that you can get around rather easily by bicycle. Rentals cost about $10 per day, and you should have no trouble locating the rental shops as you come off the boat. Moped rentals are much more expensive—at least $50 per day for a two-person vehicle. However, if you can afford it, renting one may make sense since they allow you to cover much more ground in a short period of time. Most bike rental establishments also offer mopeds.

Bus service runs from Nantucket center to Siasconset and other island beaches during the summer, or you may find it more convenient to explore the island by taxi or on a guided tour. **Barrett's Tours** at 20 Federal Street operates both a taxi service and guided tours. Call (508) 228-0174 or 800-773-0174 for information. **Nantucket Island Tours** on Straight Wharf also runs island tours regularly from May through October; tickets cost about $10 for adults, $5 for children (508-228-0334).

Lodging
In Sconset, your lodging choices are limited to **Wade Cottages** (508-257-6308), which has a three-night minimum, and the **Summer House Inn** (508-257-9976), which has a restaurant. Both overlook the ocean and offer

pleasant accommodations. Wade Cottages opens in late
May and operates through September. Room rates range
from $70 to $200. Lodging at the Summer House includes
private sitting rooms. Rates start at over $200 from mid-
June to mid-September and are less off-peak. The inn
closes for the season at the end of September.

The **Jared Coffin House** at 29 Broad Street in downtown Nantucket, probably the best-known inn on the
island, is open all year. Guest rooms are spread out
among six dwellings, the oldest dating to the 1700s. The
inn also operates a respectable restaurant, with courtyard
dining in the summertime, and a cozy bar. Dining prices
are moderate, while doubles go for $135 to $175 (508-228-
2405). The **Nesbitt Inn**, just down the block at 21 Broad
Street in a large, friendly Victorian, is reasonably priced at
$38 to $100 per night for a double (508-228-0156).

The town of Nantucket has a seemingly endless list of
bed and breakfasts, yet remarkably they fill up quickly
during the height of the summer. **Nantucket Accommodations** (508-228-9559) is a reservation service that
can help you find a room; or you can try the **Union
Street Inn** (508-228-9222 or 800-225-5116) at 7 Union
with accommodations ranging from $85 to $125. Lodgers
will not be disappointed with the quality and comfort of
18 Gardner Street (508-228-1155) where double rooms
rent for $100 to $185 per night. There is also a string of
guest houses on North Water Street convenient to the
town center, among them, the **Brass Lantern Inn**
(508-228-4064 or 800-377-6609) and the **Periwinkle
Guesthouse** (508-228-9267 or 800-992-2899). Room rates
run from $90 to $155 at the Brass Lantern, from $40 to
$130 at the Periwinkle.

There are no campgrounds on Nantucket, but **Star of
the Sea AYH Hostel** in Surfside does give budget travelers a lodging option. Dormitory-style beds rent for $10 per
night. The hostel is 3½ miles from the ferry. The hostel is
on the National Register of Historic Places, and its oceanside location is appealing. Reservations are essential (508-
228-0433). It is open April 1 through the end of October.

Dining

The **Sconset Café** (508-257-4008), in Siasconset center,
serves both lunch and dinner in addition to selling its own
cookbook. With entrées such as Indonesian grilled shrimp
and shrimp stuffed artichokes, the café offers an interesting twist to its seafood dishes that one doesn't come
across in too many New England restaurants. Lunch
entrées run around $7, dinner entrées begin at $17. The
café is only open during the summer, as is the market
around the corner where you can pick up fresh sandwiches and pasta or potato salad to take down to the
beach with you.

The **Chanticleer Inn** (508-257-6231), also in Siasconset,
specializes in French gourmet fare and is considered by
many to be the best restaurant on the island. Festive flowers and a brightly painted carousel horse greet diners in
the restaurant's garden courtyard, making outdoor dining
a must in good weather. The atmosphere, cuisine, and
service will cost you, however, as lunch entrées start
around $15, and it would be hard to sit down to dinner
for less than $40 per person.

On South Water Street, the **Atlantic Cafe** (508-228-
0570) and the **Rose & Crown** (508-228-2595), several
doors down, both offer satisfying meals in a pub atmosphere. For casual fare, there are numerous fast-food joints
on the road leading to the Steamship Authority boat dock.
One of them, **Henry's Sandwiches** on Steamboat Wharf
(508-228-0123), makes great subs. For a hearty, down-
home traditional breakfast, try the **Downeyflake** on South
Water Street (508-228-4533). They have terrific homemade
doughnuts.

Arts and Entertainment

Places like the **Rose & Crown** and **The Brotherhood**
at 23 Broad offer in-town musical entertainment. The
Windsong (508-228-6900) at the Nantucket Inn on Macy
Lane features jazz musicians, and the **Chicken Box** (508-
228-9717) on Dave Street is an informal dance club. **The
Actor's Theatre of Nantucket** performs popular plays,
concerts, and children's matinees throughout the summer

(mid-June through September). Call (508) 228-6325 for ticket information. The **Nantucket Musical Arts Society** presents Tuesday evening concerts during July and August (508-228-1287), and the **Theatre Workshop of Nantucket** is a community theater open year-round (508-228-4305).

CAPE COD

Exposed as it is to the ocean, Nantucket tends to get beaten up occasionally by raging sea storms, yet its quiet, simple life-style seems sheltered from the outside world. In contrast, the latest trends in food, fashion, and art somehow manage to make their way out to Provincetown at the tip of Cape Cod. Once it was a stopover for the pilgrims. Today the art, gay, and tourist communities all vie for space along Provincetown's harbor, making the town a hive of activity during the summer months. Today you'll make the journey from the island of Nantucket to Provincetown, enjoying the beauty of the Cape Cod National Seashore along the way.

Suggested Schedule

8:00 a.m.	Breakfast.
9:00 a.m.	Spend your last hour and a half on Nantucket visiting a sight you missed the previous day.
10:30 a.m.	Depart for Hyannis.
12:30 p.m.	Arrive in Hyannis and begin journey to Provincetown.
1:00 p.m.	Lunch in Chatham.
2:30 p.m.	Visit the Cape Cod National Seashore.
4:30 p.m.	Travel to Provincetown and check in for the night.
5:30 p.m.	Stroll down Provincetown's colorful Commercial Street, perhaps stopping in at the Provincetown Heritage Museum or Art Association Museum.
7:00 p.m.	Dinner.

Travel Route

The suggested schedule assumes that you are traveling sometime between mid-June and mid-September. If you are traveling at any other time of year, the ferry schedule from Nantucket is much more limited, so you should call

Cape Cod

either the Steamship Authority (508-228-0262) or Hy-Line
Cruises (508-778-2602) for departure times during
your visit.

From Hyannis, take Route 28 east to Orleans, stopping
in the lovely town of Chatham for lunch. If you have time,
visit the Chatham Lighthouse on Shore Road off Route 28,
or drive down seaside lanes. Some of the cape's most
beautiful homes are on the ocean in Chatham.

From Chatham, continue on Route 28 to Orleans where
Route 28 intersects with US 6. Follow US 6 to Provincetown. The Salt Pond visitor center off US 6 in Eastham is
one of the main visitor information centers for the Cape
Cod National Seashore. At Truro, Route 6A will take you
by oceanside motels and cottages if you're looking for
simple beachfront accommodations. US 6 will take you
right by the sand dunes.

Sightseeing Highlights
▲▲▲The Cape Cod National Seashore—The National Seashore stretches from the eastern half of the cape's elbow all the way out to its fingertips at Provincetown, offering the visitor miles of nature trails, beaches, and wind-sculpted sand dunes peppered with beach grass. You won't be able to cover all 27,000 acres of the seashore in one afternoon, but a ranger at the Salt Pond visitor center can send you off in the direction of Nauset Lighthouse, a good hiking trail, or a remote beach. There's a marsh trail right behind the visitor center, as well as a nature trail especially designed for the blind. You can park at Nauset Beach for $3 a day, and there is a bathhouse facility available there in season. From the nearby Coast Guard Station you can see the place where Henry Beston's "Outermost House" once stood (unfortunately, it was washed away with the extreme tides brought by the blizzard of 1978). The seashore is open to the public year-round.

▲Provincetown Art Association and Museum—Changing exhibits include works by respected American artists such as Milton Avery, as well as promising newcomers to the art scene. The museum at 460 Commercial Street is open daily from noon to 5:00 p.m., and from 7:00 p.m. to 10:00 p.m. during the summer months. Admission is $2 for adults, $1 for children, students, and seniors. Call (508) 487-1750 for off-season hours.

▲Provincetown Heritage Museum—Artifacts pertaining to the sea make up the majority of the museum's exhibits, the focal point being the 64-foot-long half-scale model of the *Rose Dorothea*, a turn-of-the-century fishing vessel. It is the largest indoor boat model in the world. Admission to the museum is $2 for adults, children under 12 free. The museum is open from 10:00 a.m. to 5:00 p.m. during the summer. It is on the corner of Commercial and Center streets.

▲Pilgrim Monument and Provincetown Museum—You will have no trouble locating the monument because, at 255 feet, it is the tallest all-granite structure in the United States. It affords marvelous views of the cape and

South Shore on clear days. Museum exhibits spotlight
outer Cape Cod history. Unfortunately, handicapped
access is limited as there is no elevator to the top of the
monument. Visitors must use ramps and stairs to climb to
the top. Admission is $5 for adults; there is no charge for
children. Open daily 9:00 a.m. to 5:00 p.m. except during
the summer months when it is open until 9:00 p.m.

Most Provincetown sights are easily accessible on foot,
but if you're worn out from hiking along the seashore, the
Provincetown Trolley Company does offer narrated
sightseeing tours. Tours leave from Town Hall on
Commercial Street about every half hour from 10:00 a.m.
to 4:00 p.m. and on the hour from 5:00 p.m. to 8:00 p.m.
during the summer. The forty-minute tour costs $6 for
adults, $5 for seniors, and $4 for children under 12.

Lodging

The Victorian **Anchor Inn** at 175 Commercial Street has a
wonderful porch for people-watching, an attractive garden
in front, and oceanview rooms that rent for about $115 in
the summer, and for $75 in the off-season (508-487-0432).
Rooms without ocean views are on the low end of the
price range, and the inn is open throughout the year. Also
open year-round is the **White Wind Inn** just across the
street. Doubles go for $45 to $110. Call (508) 487-1526 for
reservations. The **Somerset Guesthouse** on the corner of
Commercial and Pearl streets has reasonable rates at $50
to $89 (508-487-0383). All inns listed are convenient to
downtown Provincetown.

Route 6A in nearby Truro has a string of cottages and
motels on the beach. Accommodations there vary in quality but are an option if you want to stay on the beach or if
you are traveling with a family and find in-town bed and
breakfasts too expensive for your whole crew. If you
have trouble finding lodging in the area, try calling
Provincetown's lodging information number, (508) 487-
3424, for assistance. For those traveling on a tight budget,
the **Little America Hostel** in Truro has accommodations
for $10 per person per night (508-349-3889). The hostel is
only open during the summer months.

Camping

Coastal Acres Camping Court on the West Vine Street
Extension is the closest campground to downtown
Provincetown. They do have a three-night minimum stay
requirement for reservations, but you could call on the
day of your arrival and see if they have space available
(508-487-1700). Sites cost $20 for a tent and $27 for RV
hookups. The campground is open April through October.
Dune's Edge Campground off US 6 is just a little farther
from town but still convenient and borders on sand dunes
of the National Seashore (508-487-9815). Sites start at $19
per night, and the campground is open May through
September. In North Truro there are three campgrounds
you might try if Coastal Acres and Dunes Edge are full.
They are **Horton's Park** (starting at $15 per site; 508-
487-1220 or 800-252-2671), **North of Highland Camping
Area** ($16 per site; 508-487-1191), and **North Truro
Camping Area**, which is open all year ($7 per person
$14 per site minimum; 508-487-1847).

Dining

For a different sort of dining experience, try **Old Reliable
Fish House** at 229 Commercial Street (508-487-9742). It
has a mixed menu of Portuguese and Yankee specialties.
The restaurant is on the water with outdoor seating in season, and prices are reasonable. **Ciro & Sals** on Kiley
Court is known statewide for sumptuous northern Italian
creations. Prices are on the high end, and reservations
are strongly recommended (508-487-0049). The **Grand
Central Cafe** at 5 Masonic Place gives seafood a Mexican
treatment with dishes such as lobster enchiladas, shrimp
fajitas, and crab chile rellenos. Dinner prices range from
$12 to $16 (508-487-9116).

On the more traditional side, **Vorelli's** at 226 Commercial Street serves Italian and seafood dishes in a nice
atmosphere. Dinner entrées range from $14 to $18. The
restaurant also has a raw bar (508-487-2778). Also on
Commercial Street, **The Mew's**, which was once a stable
(508-487-1500), and **Pepe's** (508-487-0670) are popular for
seafood, while **Cafe Blase** (508-487-9465) serves tasty

sandwiches at moderate prices and has a pleasant sidewalk cafe in the summertime. There is no shortage of sub
shops and pizza joints in town, and ice cream lovers are
bound to be tempted by Provincetown's many ice cream
parlors.

Itinerary Options
If you have more time, the Cape Cod National Seashore
has enough beautiful coastline to occupy nature enthusiasts
and beach bums alike for many a day. There is always a
new dune to investigate. Whale watching is also an agreeable pastime in this part of the world. The *Portuguese
Princess* shuttles eager marine mammal watchers daily
from Provincetown, April through November, to view the
whales in their natural habitat. Call (508) 487-2651 or
800-442-3188 for reservations. Tickets start about $15
per person.

PLYMOUTH

In 1620, the Pilgrims actually landed in Provincetown first before settling in Plymouth because of its protected harbor. Today you'll follow the Pilgrims' path from Provincetown to Plymouth and discover how they survived that first cold winter in America.

Suggested Schedule

8:30 a.m.	Leave Provincetown for Plymouth.
11:00 a.m.	Visit Plimouth Plantation.
1:00 p.m.	Lunch.
2:00 p.m.	Visit Plymouth Rock and the *Mayflower II*.
3:00 p.m.	Visit Cranberry World, Pilgrim Hall, or other sightseeing highlight of your choice.
5:00 p.m.	Check into lodging.

Travel Route: Provincetown to Plymouth (85 miles)
From Provincetown, take US 6 to Orleans. At Orleans get on scenic Route 6A and follow it all the way to the Sagamore Bridge. Route 6A is lined with quaint Cape Cod villages, such as Barnstable and Yarmouth, where you may want to stop along the way. Brewster has lots of antique shops and several small museums including the **Cape Cod Aquarium** (open daily from 10:00 a.m. to 5:00 p.m.), the **New England Fire and History Museum** (open Monday through Friday 10:00 a.m. to 4:00 p.m., Saturday and Sunday from noon to 4:00 p.m., mid-May through mid-October, or by appointment throughout the rest of the year; adults $4.50, seniors $3.50, children 5 to 12 $2.50), and the **Cape Cod Museum of Natural History** (open Monday-Saturday from 9:30 a.m. to 4:30 p.m. and Sunday from 12:30 p.m. to 4:30 p.m. May through mid-October, closed Monday during the rest of the year; admission is $2.50 for adults, $1.50 for children). From Sagamore, take Route 3 to the Cedarville Exit (#2) and follow Route 3A north to Plymouth. Plimouth Plantation is on your left before you reach the town of Plymouth.

Sightseeing Highlights
▲▲▲Plimouth Plantation and the *Mayflower II*—
Both the plantation and the ship are run by the same non-
profit organization. The plantation is a living museum
exemplifying everyday seventeenth-century Pilgrim life
and that of nineteenth-century Native Americans in the
neighboring Wampanaog Settlement. In the Pilgrim village
of thatched cottages, costumed guides play the parts of
the original settlers tending to their farm animals, gardens,
and everyday chores. They claim to know nothing of
modern times but are happy to explain how and why
things were done in 1627. The *Mayflower II* is docked in
Plymouth Harbor adjacent to Plymouth Rock several miles
away. Since historians aren't really sure what happened to
the original *Mayflower*, this replica was built in England in
the 1950s. On board, costumed guides relate the events of
the fateful 1620 voyage, and you can see the cramped
conditions under which the Pilgrims traveled. *Mayflower II*
and Plimouth Plantation are open daily April through
November from 9:00 a.m. to 5:00 p.m. The *Mayflower II* is
open until 6:30 p.m. from late June through Labor Day.
Admission to the plantation is $12 for adults, $8 for children. Admission to the ship is $5.75 for adults, $3.75 for
children. Combination tickets are $18.50 for adults, $11
for children 5 to 12.
▲Plymouth Rock—There is nothing extraordinary about
this enshrined rock other than the fact that it symbolizes
the Pilgrims' first settlement and thus is a cornerstone of
American colonization. Visiting Plymouth Rock is probably
comparable to kissing the Blarney Stone; all true patriots
should make a pilgrimage there once in a lifetime for their
country's sake.
▲Cranberry World—Outside the museum building is a
small cranberry bog where you can see how this one of
only three native American fruits is grown. Inside there
are exhibits on how the tangy fruit is harvested and its
uses through the years. Since the museum is operated by
the Ocean Spray company, there is no charge for admission, and of course samples of cranberry refreshments are
also free. Cranberry World is located at 225 Water Street in

Plymouth and is open daily 9:30 a.m. to 5:00 p.m., May through November. The center is open until 9:00 p.m. Monday through Friday during July and August.

▲**Plymouth National Wax Museum**—Overlooking Plymouth Rock and harbor from atop Coles Hill, the museum re-creates events in Pilgrim history using wax figures. Open daily 9:00 a.m. to 5:00 p.m., March through November. Admission is $5 for adults, $2 for children.

▲**Pilgrim Hall Museum**—The museum, which is on the National Register of Historic Places, houses actual personal belongings of the Pilgrims, including Governor Bradford's Bible and Myles Standish's sword. It is located at 75 Court Street on Route 3A in the center of Plymouth. Admission is $5 for adults, $4.50 for seniors, $2 for children 6 to 15. The museum is open year-round from 9:30 a.m. to 4:30 p.m. daily, except for Christmas and New Year's Day.

▲**Cordage Park Marketplace**—The marketplace, now filled with factory outlet stores and boutiques, is of interest because it stands on the site of a nineteenth-century rope manufacturing plant. The Plymouth mill was the world's largest and employed an army of workers. The prints and photographs on display throughout the marketplace will give you some sense of the factory's magnitude. Cordage Park is on Route 3A about 1 miles north of downtown Plymouth.

▲**Pilgrim Path**—In addition to leading you to the *Mayflower II*, Plymouth Rock, and the Pilgrim Hall, this trail will lead you to other historic buildings throughout Plymouth. You'd need to spend a lot of time in Plymouth if you want to see them all, but here's a sampling of what's available:

▲**Sparrow House**, at 42 Summer Street, was built in 1640 and is the oldest house in Plymouth. Now the museum houses rotating exhibits and a craft gallery, and admission is by donation. It is open daily except Wednesday 10:00 a.m. to 5:00 p.m., late May through mid-October. The craft gallery is open through December.

The **Court House and Museum** on Town Square operated as a municipal building longer than any other court house in America. It is open daily during the summer, and admission is free. **Howland House** at 33 Sandwich Street is the only house still standing in Plymouth which an original Pilgrim actually lived in. Tours are given by costumed guides. The house is open daily from 10:00 a.m. to 5:00 p.m., late May through mid-October. Admission is $2.50 for adults, 50 cents for children.

The **Spooner House**, built in 1749, was the home of Bourne Spooner, founder of the Plymouth Cordage Company. The house remained in the Spooner family until 1954, and many of the original furnishings are on display. It is open from late May through mid-October; admission is $2.50 for adults, 50 cents for children.

The lovely **Antiquarian House** at 126 Water Street was frequented by Daniel Webster and has a number of unusual octagonally shaped rooms. It is also open from late May through mid-October and admission is charged. The **Mayflower Society Museum** is also housed in a beautiful home. It is the headquarters of the General Society of Mayflower Descendants, but nonmembers can visit the office and library Monday through Friday from 1:30 p.m. to 3:30 p.m. Admission is $2.50 for adults and 25 cents for children.

For a map and complete listing of sites along the Pilgrim Path, contact the Plymouth Area Chamber of Commerce at 91 Samoset Street, Plymouth, MA 02360.

Lodging

The Pilgrim Sands Motel, on Route 3A, is a popular lodging choice because of its oceanfront location and proximity to Plimouth Plantation. Doubles range from $44 to $108 (508-747-0900). On a smaller scale, the **Colonial House Inn** at 207 Sandwich Street (on Route 3A south of the town center) is also convenient to sights and has reasonable rates ($50 to $80). Call (508) 746-2087 for reservations. The **Sheraton Plymouth at Village Landing** at 180 Water Street is adjacent to the Village Landing Marketplace, not far from Plymouth Rock. Double rooms range from $95 to $160 per night, and it is best to make reservations several weeks ahead during the summer (800-

325-3535). The **Governor Bradford Motor Inn** is right
on Plymouth's waterfront. Rooms have refrigerators and
coffee makers and range from $44 to $117 (800-332-1620
or 508-746-6200). The **John Carver Inn** in Plymouth's
town center is run by the same people who operate the
fine Dan'l Webster Inn in Sandwich. Doubles range from
$65 to $105. Call (508) 746-7100 or (800)274-1620 for
reservations.

Camping
Indianhead Campground, off Route 3A, south of
Plymouth, is the closest camping area to Plymouth's
attractions. The campground has complete hookups and
recreational facilities including miniature golf, aquabikes,
canoes, and rowboats. Sites start at $20 per night for two.
Call (508) 888-3688 for reservations. **Myles Standish State
Forest**, about 10 miles from Plymouth off Route 58 in
South Carver, has 475 campsites plus swimming, hiking,
boating, and fishing. Sites range from $10 to $12 per night.
Call (508) 866-2526 for information.

Dining
Station One at 51 Main Street serves a variety of dishes in
an agreeable setting. The building was constructed in the
early 1900s as a fire station (508-746-1200) **McGrath's
Harbour Restaurant** (508-746-9751) overlooking the harbor in downtown Plymouth is a popular spot for seafood.
Lunch entrées range from $3.95 to $9.95, dinner entrées
from $8.95 to $13.95. Restaurants are plentiful all along
Water Street at the waterfront. There are also informal eat-
in or takeout seafood shacks out on the piers. Try **Wood's**
on Town Pier where a fried clam plate for $7.95 will easily
satisfy two hungry appetites.

THE SOUTH SHORE

Today brings you full circle to Boston, where your 22-day journey began. If you have time, drive through the pretty seaside villages of Duxbury, Hingham, and Cohasset, then perhaps visit the John F. Kennedy Library for an indepth look at a president whose youth, charisma, and promise were so influential in shaping modern history.

Suggested Schedule

8:00 a.m.	Breakfast.
9:00 a.m.	Leave Plymouth for Boston traveling along Massachusetts' South Shore.
12:00 noon	Lunch in Cohasset.
1:00 p.m.	Explore Hingham and World's End Reservation.
2:00 p.m.	Visit the Adams National Historic Site in Quincy.
3:30 p.m.	Visit the JFK Library.
5:00 p.m.	Return to Boston.

Travel Route: Plymouth to Boston (40 miles)

Today's schedule assumes you are not rushing back to catch a plane. If you are, take Route 3 north to Interstate 93 north directly to Boston. The trip will take about an hour, longer in traffic.

Should you wish to return to Boston in a more leisurely fashion, take Route 3A north from Plymouth. 3A merges with Route 3 briefly, so be sure to exit for the Duxburys at 3A to continue on the coastal route. 3A will take you through the towns of Duxbury, Marshfield, Cohasset, and Hingham, but the nicest houses and best views of the ocean are off the highway. In these towns, I recommend taking back road detours to investigate the villages more thoroughly.

True to its name, Marshfield has two wildlife sanctuaries in marshy habitats: the North River Wildlife Sanctuary and the Daniel Webster Wildlife Sanctuary. Check with the

The South Shore

ATLANTIC OCEAN

regional office of the **Massachusetts Audubon Society** at
2000 Main for details on the four sanctuaries they operate
on the South Shore (617-837-9400). In Duxbury, you
might want to seek out the **John Alden House** at 105
Alden Street, home of the famous Mayflower couple, John
and Priscilla Alden (open Tuesday through Sunday late
June through early September; admission is charged), or
the **Old Burying Ground** on Chestnut Street where Myles
Standish is buried along with other passengers from the
Mayflower. In Cohasset, be sure to drive out to the harbor.
In Hingham, there is the World's End Reservation, 250
acres of shoreline park designed by Frederick Law
Olmstead, whose work you've seen in the Boston
Public Gardens.

In Quincy, follow signs to the Adams National Historic
Site. Then return to 3A, which will take you to Interstate
93 north. To get to the Kennedy Library, take Exit 14 off
I-93 to Morrissey Boulevard. Follow signs to the library.

After visiting the library, get back on I-93 north to Boston, to the airport, or to your next destination.

Sightseeing Highlights
▲**Adams National Historic Site**—The site is actually comprised of houses at several different locations which were the homes and birthplaces of U.S. presidents John Adams and John Quincy Adams, writers Henry and Brook Adams, and envoy Charles Adams. The tour of the home at 135 Adams Street is the most worthwhile of the three. Tour guides provide in-depth historical background information to go along with family artifacts. I especially enjoyed the library. If you wish to see the birthplaces as well, the tour guides can provide you with directions. The homes are open daily 9:00 a.m. to 5:00 p.m., mid-April through mid-November. Admission is $2 for adults. Children under 16 are admitted free.

▲▲**John F. Kennedy Library**—Don't let the term "library" keep you from going because you think you're going to see nothing but books. In an imposing building designed by noted architect I. M. Pei overlooking the ocean, your visit begins with a film on Kennedy. Then it's on to the exhibits, which include Kennedy's presidential desk and a time line juxtaposing Kennedy memorabilia, events in his life, and major events of the day. More than just a tribute to one man, the library gives you a fascinating look at our recent past. It also is a thought-provoking way to end the trip since it provides you with a point of reference to judge modern America against the dreams of our founding fathers whose ideals have become apparent during the past three weeks. The library is open daily from 9:00 a.m. to 5:00 p.m., closing only for Thanksgiving, Christmas, and New Year's Day. The last film of the day starts at 3:50 p.m. Admission is $3.50 for adults and $2 for seniors. Children under 16 are admitted free.

Dining
Kimball's by the Sea at 124 Elm Street overlooking the water in Cohasset is known for its seafood and might be a

good place to stop for lunch if you're not picnicking
(617-383-6650).

Boston

Boston will seem like an old friend as the city's skyline
comes into view upon your return. The city is well worth
getting to know better if prior obligations are not calling
you home. If you must leave the area, New England's
charms are certain to beckon you back for another visit.

FESTIVALS AND EVENTS

Each New England state has its share of folk festivals ranging from arts and crafts fairs to lobsterfests. These regional events are a fun way to soak up local culture, and I've listed some of the area's best and most colorful below.

Connecticut
May
Lobsterfest, Mystic Seaport Museum, Mystic
June
Sea Music Festival, Mystic Seaport
August
Connecticut River Raft Race, Haddam Meadows State Park, Haddam
Native American Festival, Haddam Meadows State Park, Haddam
September
Harbor Festival, New London
October
Chowderfest, Mystic Seaport Museum, Mystic
December
First Night, Hartford
Victorian Christmas, Gillette Castle State Park, Hadlyme
Christmas at Mystic Seaport, Mystic

Write Tourist Events, Department of Economic Development, 865 Brook Street, Rocky Hill, CT 06067, for a complete list of Connecticut events.

Maine
January
New Year's Eve Celebration, Portland
Happy New Year's Champagne Cup, Sunday River Ski Area, Bethel
June
Old Port Festival, Old Port, Portland
July
Seafood Festival, Bar Harbor
Great Schooner Race, Rockland Harbor, Rockland

Annual Dulcimer Festival, Bar Harbor
Rockport Folk Festival, Rockport
Arcady Music Festival, Mt. Desert
August
Lobster Festival, Rockland
Maine Arts Festival, Portland
December
Christmas Prelude, Kennebunkport

Contact the Maine Publicity Bureau at 97 Winthrop Street,
   Hallowell, ME 04347 (207-289-2423), for the most current
   events calendar.

Massachusetts
January
First Night New Year's Eve Celebration, Boston
March
St. Patrick's Day Parade, South Boston
April
The Boston Marathon, Boston
Daffodil Festival, Nantucket
Reenactment of Paul Revere's Ride, Boston
Reenactment of the Battle of Lexington and Concord,
   Lexington
May
Art Newbury Street, Boston
Salem Seaport Festival, Salem
Wool Days, Sturbridge Village
Boston Kite Festival, Franklin Park, Boston
June
Dairy Festival, Boston
Cape Cod Chowderfest, Hyannis
July
Boston Pops Concert and Fourth of July Fireworks
   Display, The Esplanade, Boston
Bastille Day, Marlborough Street, Boston
Chowderfest, Boston
Tisbury Street Fair, Martha's Vineyard
Edgartown Regatta, Martha's Vineyard
Marblehead Race Week, Marblehead
Stockbridge Antique Show, Stockbridge

Yankee Homecoming Days, Newburyport
U.S.S. Constitution Turnaround, Boston
Harborfest, Boston
August
Annual Festival of Shaker Crafts and Industries, Hancock
  Shaker Village
Mayflower Lobster Festival, Plymouth
Marshfield Fair, Marshfield
September
Cambridge River Festival, Cambridge
Eastern States Exposition, West Springfield
Bourne Scallop Festival, Buzzard's Bay
Essex Clamfest, Essex
Old Deerfield Craft Fair, Deerfield
Cranberry Festival, Harwich
Waterfront Festival, Newburyport
Cape Ann Road Race, Gloucester
October
Head of the Charles Regatta, Charles River, Cambridge
Mt.Greylock Ramble, Adams
November
Hammond Castle Museum Medieval Feast, Gloucester
Plimouth Plantation Thanksgiving Day, Plymouth
December
Christmas Stroll, Nantucket
Chowderfest, Vineyard Haven, Martha's Vineyard
Christmas at Hancock Shaker Village, Hancock

For more information on "Bay state" festivals, contact the
  Commonwealth of Massachusetts Office of Travel and
  Tourism, 100 Cambridge Street, 13th Floor, Boston, MA
  02202.

New Hampshire
February
Dartmouth Winter Carnival, Hanover
Chocolate Festival, Mt. Cranmore, North Conway
April
Old Man of the Mountain Race, Attitash, Bartlett
May
Mountainfest, Mt. Washington Valley

June
Mt. Washington Road Race, Mt. Washington
Old Timer's Fair, Hanover
Annual Fiddler's Contest, Lincoln
Jazz Festival, Portsmouth
July
Annual Hayseed Bluegrass Festival, Franconia
Mid-summer Arts and Crafts Fair, Loon Mountain, Lincoln
September
World Mud Bowl Championships, Hog Coliseum, North
   Conway
Highland Games, Loon Mountain, Lincoln
October
Fall Foliage Festival, Loon Mountain, Lincoln
December
Candlelight Stroll, Strawberry Banke, Portsmouth

For more detailed information on New Hampshire festivals, contact the State of New Hampshire, Office of
   Vacation Travel, P.O. Box 856-RC, Concord, NH 03301
   (603-271-2666).

Rhode Island
January
Polar Bears Dip, New Year's Day, Newport Beach,
   Newport
June
Block Island Race Week, Block Island
Outdoor Art Festival, Newport
Taste of Block Island Seafood Festival, Block Island
Great Chowder Cook-off, Newport Yachting Center
July
Black Ships Festival, Newport
Newport Music Festival, Newport Mansions
Virginia Slims Tennis Tournament, Newport Casino,
   Newport
August
JVC Jazz Festival at Newport, Fort Adams
Great Gatsby Ball, Rosecliff, Newport
September
Newport International Boat Show, Newport

November
Block Island's Annual Shopping Stroll, Block Island
December
Christmas in Newport, Newport

Call or write the Newport Tourism and Convention
Authority, P.O. Box 782, Newport, RI 02840
(401-849-8048), for a free descriptive brochure of
Newport County's numerous cultural events.

Vermont
March
Maple Festival, Woodstock
April
Festival of Quilts, Rutland
May
Lilac Sunday, Shelburne Museum, Shelburne
Spring Farm Festival, Billings Farm Museum, Woodstock
June
Hot Air Balloon Festival, Quechee
Cow Appreciation Day, Billing Farm Museum, Woodstock
July
Vermont Lumberjack Roundup, Rutland
Summer Festival and Craft Fair, Woodstock
August
Fools-A-Float, Burlington
Scottish Festival, Quechee
Bennington Battle Day Weekend, Bennington
September
Vermont State Fair, Rutland
Shelburne Harvest Festival, Shelburne
Stratton Arts Festival, Stratton Mountain
December
Wassail Festival, Woodstock
Festival of Christmas Trees, Stowe

The Vermont Chamber of Commerce, Box 37, Montpelier,
VT 05601 (802-223-3443), can provide you with
additional information about ongoing activities and
events in the state.

Skiing in New England is as popular with natives as leaf-peeping is with travelers. Skiing can be an invigorating way to extend your vacation and supplement the itinerary, if you're visiting the region during the winter months when many other sightseeing attractions are closed. The following list is comprised of ski areas convenient to the main *2 to 22 Days in New England* route.

Maine
Snow Bowl in Camden (207-236-3438) is a small mountain offering pleasant skiing for the whole family. **Sunday River** in Bethel (207-824-2187) is more extensive with fifty trails and a 1,854-foot vertical drop.

Massachusetts
Butternut Basin in Great Barrington (413-528-2000), **Catamount** in South Egremont (413-528-1262), **Jiminy Peak** in Hancock (413-738-5500), and **Brodie Mountain** in New Ashford (413-443-4752) are all in the Berkshire region of the state and provide skiing terrain for all levels of ability. Brodie has the greatest vertical drop at 1,250 feet, while Catamount straddles the Massachusetts and New York border. Brodie and Butternut both have cross-country trails as well.

New Hampshire
The Mt. Washington valley is heavily populated with ski areas. **Black Mountain** in Jackson (603-383-4490) and **Mt. Cranmore** in North Conway (603-356-5543) are good family mountains since they cater to all levels of ability. Mt. Cranmore's skimobile tramway is a godsend to those scared of chair lifts. **Attitash** in Bartlett (603-374-2368 or 800-862-1600), **Wildcat** opposite the Mt. Washington Auto Road (603-466-3326), **Cannon** in Franconia (603-823-5563), and **Loon Mountain** in Lincoln (603-745-8111) offer experienced skiers more of a challenge. Wildcat and Loon both have gondolas, and Cannon operates an aerial

tramway. **Bretton Woods** near the cog railway to the top of Mt. Washington is best known for its cross-country trails (603-278-5000). The town of Jackson is also a major cross-country center; contact the Jackson Ski Touring Foundation at (603) 383-9355 for information.

Tuckerman's Ravine at Pinkham Notch is only for the most adventurous and expert skiers. There are no lifts so skiers must hike two and a half miles. Check with the White Mountain National Forest Service before trying to tackle the ravine. Because of avalanche danger in winter, only spring skiing is allowed (603-466-2725).

Vermont

Killington (802-773-1500), with 100 trails and a 3,081-foot vertical drop, is the largest ski area discussed here. Nearby **Pico** (802-775-4345), outside of Rutland, is also an enjoyable place to ski. **Bromley** in Manchester (802-824-5522) has 35 trails, and **Stratton** (802-297-2200), 20 minutes away, is a popular ski resort as well.

As lift tickets vary from mountain to mountain, and weather conditions vary from day to day, it is best to call ahead for the most up-to-date information during your visit. Dress warmly! Western skiers may be caught off-guard by the Northeast's sometimes frigid temperatures.

INDEX

Other Books from John Muir Publications

Asia Through the Back Door, 4th ed., 400 pp. $16.95 (available 7/93)

Belize: A Natural Destination, 336 pp. $16.95

Costa Rica: A Natural Destination, 2nd ed., 310 pp. $16.95

Elderhostels: The Students' Choice, 2nd ed., 304 pp. $15.95

Environmental Vacations: Volunteer Projects to Save the Planet, 2nd ed., 248 pp. $16.95

Europe 101: History & Art for the Traveler, 4th ed., 350 pp. $15.95

Europe Through the Back Door, 11th ed., 432 pp. $17.95

Europe Through the Back Door Phrase Book: French, 160 pp. $4.95

Europe Through the Back Door Phrase Book: German, 160 pp. $4.95

Europe Through the Back Door Phrase Book: Italian, 168 pp. $4.95

Europe Through the Back Door Phrase Book: Spanish & Portuguese, 288 pp. $4.95

A Foreign Visitor's Guide to America, 224 pp. $12.95

Great Cities of Eastern Europe, 256 pp. $16.95

Guatemala: A Natural Destination, 336 pp. $16.95

Indian America: A Traveler's Companion, 4th ed., 448 pp. $17.95 (available 7/93)

Interior Furnishings Southwest, 256 pp. $19.95

Mona Winks: Self-Guided Tours of Europe's Top Museums, 2nd ed., 448 pp. $16.95

Opera! The Guide to Western Europe's Great Houses, 296 pp. $18.95

Paintbrushes and Pistols: How the Taos Artists Sold the West, 288 pp. $17.95

The People's Guide to Mexico, 9th ed., 608 pp. $18.95

Ranch Vacations: The Complete Guide to Guest and Resort, Fly-Fishing, and Cross-Country Skiing Ranches, 2nd ed., 396 pp. $18.95

The Shopper's Guide to Art and Crafts in the Hawaiian Islands, 272 pp. $13.95

The Shopper's Guide to Mexico, 224 pp. $9.95

Understanding Europeans, 272 pp. $14.95

Undiscovered Islands of the Caribbean, 3rd ed., 288 pp. $14.95

Undiscovered Islands of the Mediterranean, 2nd ed., 224 pp. $13.95

Undiscovered Islands of the U.S. and Canadian West Coast, 288 pp. $12.95

Unique Colorado, 112 pp. $10.95 (available 6/93)
Unique Florida, 112 pp. $10.95 (available 7/93)
Unique New Mexico, 112 pp. $10.95 (available 6/93)
A Viewer's Guide to Art: A Glossary of Gods, People, and Creatures, 144 pp. $10.95
The Visitor's Guide to the Birds of the Eastern National Parks: United States and Canada, 410 pp. $15.95

2 to 22 Days Series
Each title offers 22 flexible daily itineraries useful for planning vacations of any length. Aside from valuable general information, included are "must see" attractions *and* hidden "jewels."

2 to 22 Days in the American Southwest, 1993 ed., 176 pp. $10.95

2 to 22 Days in Asia, 1993 ed., 176 pp. $9.95

2 to 22 Days in Australia, 1993 ed., 192 pp. $9.95

2 to 22 Days in California, 1993 ed., 192 pp. $9.95

2 to 22 Days in Europe, 1993 ed., 288 pp. $13.95

2 to 22 Days in Florida, 1993 ed., 192 pp. $10.95

2 to 22 Days in France, 1993 ed., 192 pp. $10.95

2 to 22 Days in Germany, Austria, & Switzerland, 1993 ed., 224 pp. $10.95

2 to 22 Days in Great Britain, 1993 ed., 192 pp. $10.95

2 to 22 Days Around the Great Lakes, 1993 ed., 192 pp. $10.95

2 to 22 Days in Hawaii, 1993 ed., 192 pp. $9.95

2 to 22 Days in Italy, 208 pp. $10.95

2 to 22 Days in New England, 1993 ed., 192 pp. $10.95

2 to 22 Days in New Zealand, 1993 ed., 192 pp. $9.95

2 to 22 Days in Norway, Sweden, & Denmark, 1993 ed., 192 pp. $10.95

2 to 22 Days in the Pacific Northwest, 1993 ed., 192 pp. $10.95

2 to 22 Days in the Rockies, 1993 ed., 192 pp. $10.95

2 to 22 Days in Spain & Portugal, 192 pp. $10.95

2 to 22 Days in Texas, 1993 ed., 192 pp. $9.95

2 to 22 Days in Thailand, 1993 ed., 180 pp. $9.95
22 Days (or More) Around the World, 1993 ed., 264 pp. $12.95

Automotive Titles
How to Keep Your VW Alive, 15th ed., 464 pp. $21.95
How to Keep Your Subaru Alive 480 pp. $21.95
How to Keep Your Toyota Pickup Alive 392 pp. $21.95
How to Keep Your Datsun/Nissan Alive 544 pp. $21.95
The Greaseless Guide to Car Care Confidence, 224 pp. $14.95
Off-Road Emergency Repair & Survival, 160 pp. $9.95

TITLES FOR YOUNG READERS AGES 8 AND UP

"Kidding Around" Travel Guides for Young Readers
All the "Kidding Around" Travel guides are 64 pages and $9.95
paper, except for **Kidding Around Spain** and **Kidding Around
the National Parks of the Southwest**, which are 108 pages
and $12.95 paper.

Kidding Around Atlanta
Kidding Around Boston, 2nd ed.
Kidding Around Chicago, 2nd ed.
Kidding Around the Hawaiian Islands
Kidding Around London
Kidding Around Los Angeles
Kidding Around the National Parks of the Southwest
Kidding Around New York City, 2nd ed.
Kidding Around Paris
Kidding Around Philadelphia
Kidding Around San Diego
Kidding Around San Francisco
Kidding Around Santa Fe
Kidding Around Seattle
Kidding Around Spain
Kidding Around Washington, D.C., 2nd ed.

"Extremely Weird" Series for Young Readers. Written by
Sarah Lovett, each is 48 pages and $9.95 paper.
Extremely Weird Bats
Extremely Weird Birds
Extremely Weird Endangered Species
Extremely Weird Fishes
Extremely Weird Frogs
Extremely Weird Insects
Extremely Weird Mammals (available 8/93)
Extremely Weird Micro Monsters (available 8/93)
Extremely Weird Primates
Extremely Weird Reptiles
Extremely Weird Sea Creatures
Extremely Weird Snakes (available 8/93)
Extremely Weird Spiders

"Masters of Motion" Series for Young Readers. Each title is
48 pages and $9.95 paper.
How to Drive an Indy Race Car
How to Fly a 747
How to Fly the Space Shuttle

"X-ray Vision" Series for Young Readers. Each title is 48
pages and $9.95 paper.
Looking Inside Cartoon Animation
Looking Inside Sports Aerodynamics

Looking Inside the Brain
Looking Inside Sunken Treasure
Looking Inside Telescopes and the Night Sky

Multicultural Titles for Young Readers
Native Artists of North America, 48 pp. $14.95 hardcover
The Indian Way: Learning to Communicate with Mother Earth, 114 pp. $9.95
The Kids' Environment Book: What's Awry and Why, 192 pp. $13.95
Kids Explore America's African-American Heritage, 112 pp. $8.95
Kids Explore America's Hispanic Heritage, 112 pp. $7.95

Environmental Titles for Young Readers
Rads, Ergs, and Cheeseburgers: The Kids' Guide to Energy and the Environment, 108 pp. $12.95
Habitats: Where the Wild Things Live, 48 pp. $9.95
The Kids' Environment Book: What's Awry and Why, 192 pp. $13.95

Ordering Information
Please check your local bookstore for our books, or call 1-800-888-7504 to order direct from us. All orders are shipped via UPS; see chart below to calculate your shipping charge to U.S. destinations. **No P.O. Boxes please; we must have a street address to ensure delivery.** If the book you request is not available, we will hold your check until we can ship it. For-eign orders will be shipped surface rate unless otherwise requested; please enclose $3.00 for the first item and $1.00 for each additional item.

For U.S. Orders Totaling	Add
Up to $15.00	$4.25
$15.01 to $45.00	$5.25
$45.01 to $75.00	$6.25
$75.01 or more	$7.25

Methods of Payment
Check, money order, American Express, MasterCard, or Visa. We cannot be responsible for cash sent through the mail. For credit card orders, include your card number, expiration date, and your signature, or call (800) 888-7504. American Express card orders can be shipped only to billing address of card-holder. Sorry, no C.O.D.'s. Residents of sunny New Mexico, add 6.125% tax to total.

Address all orders and inquiries to:
John Muir Publications
P.O. Box 613
Santa Fe, NM 87504
(505) 982-4078
(800) 888-7504